"Fantastic! The auditorium was jam-packed. They were sitting in the aisles!" "You were inspirational!" "You have such strengths as a presenter and it really connected!" "You had a positive impact!" "Great Talk!" —Harvard Business School

"What a dynamic speaker!" —Stryker Medical Devices

"Joe Girard's Guinness World Record sales achievement is one of its premier examples in its story *The Art of Selling*." —*Fortune Magazine*

"I thoroughly enjoyed reading the book. It was an inspiration of 'can do' and believing in oneself and reading about other successes and realizing how we have the ability to succeed. It was fabulous." —Debra J. Fields, chairman, Mrs. Fields Cookies

"You most definitely made a major positive impact on our people" —Ingersoll-Rand

"Girard captures the essence of rising to the top in any endeavor: Set ambitious goals and visualize success, work hard, persevere, and stick to your principles." —Mary Kay Ash, founder and chairman emeritus, Mary Kay Cosmetics, Inc.

"Loved Joe's enthusiastic, catching style." —General Electric

"Joe Girard is not only master salesman but master teacher. He has the uncanny ability to communicate to you the secrets of how he did it himself." —Kemmons Wilson, founder, Holiday Inn

"An absolute turn-on for our salesmen . . . bar none!" —PPG Industries

"It takes guts to be an entrepreneur. In that quest, Joe Girard's riveting book will empower you to become tomorrow's entrepreneurial legend." —Warren E. Avis, founder, Avis Rent-A-Car

"Delivery was obviously a big hit; upbeat, positive, and nicely tailored." —Allstate Insurance

"Fabulous! We definitely overachieved our objective!" —IBM

"The consummate salesman!" —*Forbes Magazine*

"Joe's presentation was electric!" —Bell Canada

"You are truly #1!" —John Deere and Co.

"Joe Girard is something special." —*Newsweek*

Books by Joe Girard

How to Sell Yourself
How to Sell Anything to Anybody
How to Close Every Sale
Mastering Your Way to the Top
Life's 13 Rules

how to CLOSE EVERY SALE

JOE GIRARD

with Robert L. Shook

BUSINESS PLUS

NEW YORK   BOSTON

Business Plus
Hachette Book Group
237 Park Avenue
New York, NY 10017

www.HachetteBookGroup.com

Printed in the United States of America

First Edition: September 1989
Reissued: June 2002
30 29 28 27 26 25 24 23 22

Business Plus is an imprint of Grand Central Publishing.
The Business Plus name and logo are trademarks of Hachette Book Group, Inc.

The publisher is not responsible for websites (or their content) that are not owned by the publisher.

The Hachette Speakers Bureau provides a wide range of authors for speaking events. To find out more, go to www.hachettespeakersbureau.com or call (866) 376-6591.

Library of Congress Cataloging-in-Publication Data
Girard, Joe.
    How to close every sale / by Joe Girard & Robert L. Shook.
    p. cm.
    ISBN 978-0-446-38929-7
    1. Selling. I. Shook, Robert L., 1938–   II. Title.
HF5438.25G.57   1989
658.8'5—dc20
                                   89-31395
                                   CIP

Cover design by Brigid Pearson

Dedicated to my great wife Kitty
With love and admiration

CONTENTS

how to
CLOSE
EVERY
SALE

INTRODUCTION

A few years ago, I wrote a book called *How to Sell Yourself*, so I'll practice what I preach and sell you right up front on why I'm qualified to write this book. For starters, the *Guinness Book of World Records* listed me as the "World's Greatest Salesman" for having sold more than 13,000 cars in a fifteen-year period. It's considered the all-time record in retail selling of big-ticket items, and it's what I call belly-to-belly selling. There were no fleet sales and no automobile leases. I sold each car at retail, one at a time!

Since leaving the automobile industry, I've authored four books on selling, and I've spoken to groups of people all over the world about how I made all of those sales. I've spoken to all kinds of audiences—insurance agents, real estate agents, automobile dealers—you name a group of salespeople, and chances are good they've heard me speak.

It doesn't matter where I speak, audience members invariably ask the same question: "What's your secret, Joe? Tell us how you closed all of those sales."

There's no doubt that closing sales is the one subject that salespeople want to hear about in particular. And for good reason. This is the area in selling where the most difficulty occurs. After all, it's one thing to demonstrate how a spanking-new car drives, or to show a beautiful suburban home, but it's another to get prospects to put their John Hancocks on the dotted line and to part with their hard-earned money! The task becomes even tougher when the customer has a brother-in-law in the same business and wants to talk it over with him, or wants to shop around before making his or her decision. These are just two excuses you will probably hear while pitching day in and day out. As a matter of fact, I'm sure you've heard enough excuses on your own to hear them in your sleep!

Closing a sale is by far the most crucial part of the sales presentation. To put it bluntly, if you don't close the sale, you haven't accomplished your main objective. Look at it this way: Both the prospect's and your time are wasted if the sale isn't closed because no benefit is derived from your product or your service. Sure, the prospect learned some facts he might not have known before your call, but without a completed sales transaction, no money is exchanged, and neither you nor your company have been remunerated for your time and effort. You struck out. Pure and simple.

It's no wonder there's so much interest in closing sales. *It's what you, as a salesperson, are paid to do!* So don't ever fool yourself into believing that your job is to give sales presentations, no matter what the consequences. You can demonstrate your product from now until doomsday, but each time you don't close a sale, you've failed at your job. I hear a lot of salespeople say they're actually happy each time they get a no. I don't believe it. How can people be happy when they get rejected? I'm sure they're just rationalizing when they say "each no means I'm that much closer to a yes." But being happy when they lose a sale? That's absurd. Always remember: *Nothing happens until something is sold.* And nothing is sold until a sale is closed.

In our profession, closing the sale is the moment of truth. Over the years, I've seen an army of salespeople give the most beautiful presentations. They did everything by the book. Everything, that is, but the close.

As you read my message, you'll discover that closing a sale doesn't happen only at the end of your presentation. It is true, however, that the moment of truth occurs when the prospect consents to part with his or her money in exchange for your product or service. So for good reason, novice salespeople identify this response as the close of the sale—it is unquestionably the pinnacle of your sales presentation. But closing a sale is far more complex and involves everything from selling yourself to properly answering your prospect's objections. Asking for an order simply is not enough, no matter how effectively you do the asking. You must create the need for your product, and you must create a desire to own it. The prospect must believe that your product has more value than his or her money. As you'll learn throughout the pages of this book, the close of the sale is dependent upon the effectiveness of other parts of your presentation.

I'm going to tell you how to close every sale, and what I have to say is based on experience, not some theory conceived by somebody in a high-and-mighty ivory tower. You see, I've been there, and I've paid my dues. I've been out there knee-deep in the trenches. I had to close sales, or my family didn't eat. My survival depended on it.

Now, there is a lot about closing sales I'll tell you that I won't take credit for. You see, when I started my sales career, I wasn't too proud to learn from any available source so I could sell more cars. I picked the brains of every salesperson I met whenever I thought there was something worthwhile to learn. And I read books, magazine articles, and listened to cassette tapes about selling. Then I chose what I felt would work best for me. I took a little from this guy, and a little from somebody else, and gradually I refined it until I felt comfortable with it. I believe what eventually evolved is uniquely Joe Girard—but keep in mind, I didn't have to reinvent the wheel to succeed. Thankfully, you don't either to become a top producer.

You may be wondering what you can learn from me because your product is unrelated to the automobile industry. As you'll discover when you read this book, a good salesperson can sell any product. The reason is that you sell to people, and people are people—and they buy people, not products. So, what I tell you is transferable to whatever you sell, too.

As the great U.S. Supreme Court justice Oliver Wendell Holmes once said, "Many times, an idea grows better when transplanted into another mind than in the one where it sprang up." So I challenge you to take my ideas and make them work even better for you than they did for me.

Now perhaps you're thinking: "Is Joe Girard really serious about telling me how to close *every* sale?" I'm dead serious. If I weren't, I wouldn't have titled this book "How to Close *Every* Sale."

1
OVERCOMING SALES RESISTANCE

I won't keep it a secret. The vast majority of people don't like being sold. They have a built-in resistance to salespeople. In fact, if they had their choice, they would prefer it if salespeople *never* called on them.

Don't panic. I'm speaking in generalities. Don't interpret this to mean that nobody likes to be sold, nor should you think that all prospects will resist you. You must not conclude that you're automatically behind the eight ball every time you make a sales call. If you're good at your job, there will be more than enough people who will buy your product or services, enough so you can enjoy immense success in your sales career.

Let me make myself clear by saying that the last thing I want to do is begin this book by generating negative thoughts about selling. It is important, however, that we're on the same wavelength. And contrary to what some sales managers preach, you and I know that people don't like aggressive and overbearing salespeople barging into their homes and offices like gangbusters. In fact, most people go out of their way to avoid the experience. So let's not have any false illusions that a lot of people are out there waiting with open arms for you to sell them your wares. It doesn't work that way and it never will. It's not supposed to. If selling were that easy, you'd be reduced to an order-taker and your company would reduce your commissions.

I believe a realistic approach to selling must be taken, and with this in mind, you must understand that people have a variety of reasons for resisting sales. To overcome such resistance, you'd better understand this mindset.

A POOR IMAGE

Let's face it. In spite of the many professional salespeople in this world today, those of us in sales have a poor public image. What comes to *your* mind when you think of the "typical" salesperson? To level with you, even I (and I should know better) form this mental picture of a loud guy wearing a checkered suit on his way to the racetrack. You know the type, the fast talker with the forked tongue. And if I think this way, imagine what other people are thinking.

Unfortunately, it's part of our American culture to perceive salespeople as unscrupulous and scheming—it dates back to when medicine men sold snake oil to the Western pioneers. "I'll tell you what I'm gonna do!" was their pitch, and a leery and suspicious young nation soon realized that salespeople seldom delivered on their promises. The Latin words *caveat emptor* ("let the buyer beware") were inscribed in our early textbooks, warning us not to trust the seller.

The snake-oil-peddler image was perpetuated by stage and screen portrayals of fast-talking, joke-telling, and otherwise seedy and obnoxious characters. Even one of the country's greatest showmen, P. T. Barnum, was quoted as saying, "There's a sucker born every minute." While Barnum, of Barnum & Bailey Circus fame, vehemently denied making the remark, it remains a commonly used phrase to this day. In a quick review of American literature, the characters who immediately come to mind are Willy Loman from *Death of a Salesman* and Clark Gable's slick-talking adman in *The Hucksters*. Then there's Professor Harold Hill from *The Music Man*, and more recently we have Danny DeVito and Richard Dreyfuss as pathetic pitchmen in *Tinmen*. Not a single desirable character comes to mind when I think of salespeople in American literature. To my knowledge, there are no salespeople of yesteryear that a young person can use as a positive role model.

I don't intend to pass judgment on whether the prevailing image is based on fact or myth. I do know, however, that those men and women who served as our forefathers in the sales field passed down a heritage that created many hurdles for us to overcome. In my particular field, for instance, cars were sold much like horses were one hundred years ago. In fact, Americans still "horse-trade" when buying cars. At present, few people buy a car at sticker price. But in almost all other retail selling, the list price is not negotiable. For instance, you wouldn't walk into a store such as Macy's or Bloomingdale's and say, "Twenty dollars for that shirt? I'll give you fifteen." But it's an American tradition to bargain for a car—and if it goes against your grain to haggle over the price, you'll surely get ripped off.

I mention the car business so you'll know what I was up against. I had to overcome many obstacles connected with the car salesmen's poor image. Personally, I learned to run around the obstacles so I wouldn't stumble over them. These same hurdles later served as roadblocks for my competition. I believe a good salesperson must take all disadvantages and turn them into challenges that later become advantages. So when people came into my showroom with their guards up, expecting to encounter a slick and shifty car salesman, there was Joe Girard projecting a far different image from what they anticipated. That's because I wanted to help them, and I wanted to sell them what was good for them. My sincerity and conviction came across, and soon their sales resistance disappeared. As a consequence, I was viewed as being different. "Joe, you're not like the other car salesmen. I *like* doing business with you."

So the poor image that people have about salespeople doesn't have to be the one they have about you. When you're able to turn it around, it becomes your advantage because you become elevated to a level far above your competition.

THE US/THEM RELATIONSHIP

Too often, sales presentations become contests between sellers and buyers. The two parties are pitted against each other. If the salesperson makes the sale, he wins and the buyer loses. And vice versa. In other words, an "us versus them" relationship exists in which the salesperson is viewed as an opponent rather than a teammate or an ally.

Frequently, prospects think that salespeople are out to take advantage of them, so they become defensive, and throughout the presentation they concentrate on how to resist the close. It becomes a matter of self-preservation. They don't want to be manipulated into buying, even if they truly need the product and would realize an exceptional value by buying it.

Sadly, many salespeople also think of selling as a battle during which they match wits against the prospects, and if successful, they win. They view good salesmanship as gamesmanship. To these individuals, a sale represents a conquest. They become the victors and the customer is the conquered.

Frankly, I can't think of a worse scenario. When you position yourself as a foe of the prospect, you work against him instead of working *with* him. Remember that you're both on the same team, and when a sale is made, both the seller and the buyer win.

You must think in terms of how you can help your prospect by guiding him to make the right decision. Each time a person entered my dealer's showroom, I viewed it as an opportunity to help somebody buy a car. I always believed this was why the customer walked in the door. After all, people don't go to automobile dealerships unless they have such an interest. Similarly, they call stockbrokers because they're interested in investments, and they call real estate brokers because they're interested in buying and listing properties. When you think about selling in this light, you can't be the prospect's opponent; you're working on the same team.

Take, for example, an industrial salesperson who sells heavy machinery to large manufacturing companies. He must view his relationship with a customer as a partnership. He sees selling as more than a one-time-call situation. Over a period of time, he develops an understanding of each customer so that a substantial long-term relationship is established.

When this salesperson sells several million dollars' worth of machinery to the customer, his firm's marketing and technical people must also participate in the selling effort. Company engineers might also spend several weeks on the customer's site to lay out the equipment needed and make plans for its installation. They must also present a cost/benefit recommendation covering several years. A proper presentation involves hundreds of hours with the seller's people working closely with the buyer's organization. Eventually, the customer has a feeling that the two firms are working in a joint venture for his benefit. When this is accomplished, the highest level of customer satisfaction exists.

Likewise, a commercial real estate agent conveys the same feeling with his or her clients. And so does a stockbroker and a life insurance agent. It doesn't make any difference what you sell. When you truly want to serve your customer, he or she knows it and you'll overcome sales resistance. And I believe that this kind of a selling environment must be developed early in the presentation. If you fail to create it, you will come across as an opponent, and you'll be in for a real battle when it's time to close the sale. In all likelihood, it will be a battle with no winners.

PREVIOUSLY BAD EXPERIENCES WITH SALESPEOPLE

Everyone has had his or her share of bad experiences with salespeople who are unprofessional, insensitive, manipulative, double-dealing, and swindling. Harsh words, perhaps, but accurate. Sooner or later, everybody runs into one of these guys who give the rest of us a bum rap.

What's more, their shabby tactics cause many prospects to become anxious and gun-shy even when called on by a professional salesperson. You must realize that people aren't instinctually resistant to salespeople and certainly are not born with this attitude.

I'm no different from anyone else. I've met head-on with a number of obnoxious and pushy salespeople who tried to manipulate and intimidate me into buying their products. And I've been the sucker of sales presentations offering unbelievable pie-in-the-sky deals. And if I can be had by a fast-talking, wheeling-and-dealing pitchman, you better believe me when I tell you *everyone* has gone through the wringer. It's hard to imagine anyone who hasn't felt the heat and discomfort of a shyster at one time or another.

Yet everything is relative. So take my advice and turn the tables around. Create an atmosphere in which the prospect will find you congenial, informative, and professional. Imagine the pleasant relief it will be to the prospect who expects a round of browbeating and double-talking. The prospect's previously bad experiences make us good guys look all the better! That's why when I tell people to "enjoy the experience of doing business with Joe Girard," they soon know exactly what I mean.

THE PROSPECT'S TIME IS VALUABLE

Every salesperson has had it drilled into his or her skull that time is money and should be valued accordingly. So I won't give you another lecture on time management. Instead, I'll emphasize the importance of also realizing the value of your *prospect's* time.

Now that's a switch, isn't it? Too often, salespeople are so wrapped up in what they've been told in sales meetings about spending their time wisely that *they fail to consider that their customers think the same way!*

Frequently a salesperson gets shot out of the saddle before getting his foot in the door because he was thoughtless about the value of the prospect's time. Look at it this way: The best prospects are those who can afford to buy your product. And generally, people with money accumulated their wealth because they make the best use of their time. Yes, I'll say it again: Time is money. When Willie Sutton, the famous bank robber, was asked why he robbed banks, he replied: "Because that's where the money is." For the same reason, you want to give sales presentations to people who value their time.

To accomplish this, you must respect their time and understand how protective they are of it. Successful professional and business people are incredibly busy and generally have "gatekeepers" who are instructed to screen salespeople, to weed out those who have not tried to call ahead for an appointment, and to allow only the one-in-a-dozen or so past the gate and into the boss's chambers. Gatekeepers are given this assignment because their bosses are swamped with meetings, telephone calls, and visitors—especially salespeople. If top executives and business owners listened to everybody who called on them, they'd accomplish nothing else with their time. Still, there are times when they must grant audiences with salespeople. All too often, they must rely on information provided by salespeople to keep abreast of the latest developments. So even with their busy schedules, some time must be set aside for *important* sales calls. I always believed that time spent with Joe Girard was time put to good use, and I was certain that my call was one of the most important appointments my prospects should schedule with salespeople.

However, I fully appreciated how other people valued their time, and as a consequence, I always attempted to sell by appointment. You may be thinking, "A car salesman working by appointment?" Yes, and admittedly it's unusual in my business. But I did it for good reason. It not only enabled me to make the best use of my time, but it also allowed my customers to allot enough time to buy a car from me. After all, I didn't see much point in giving a partial sales presentation and in the middle of my close be told: "I'm sorry, but I have to get back to my office, Joe. I'll stop in to see you in a few days."

I started working by appointment about three years after I got into the business. I worked just like an attorney or doctor, and it made me look professional and important. On rare occasions, appointments would back up and they'd have to wait for as long as an hour. So I'd tell them, "The longer you wait, the cheaper I get." I'd explain that because I worked on volume, I only needed a small profit to make a good living, and this seemed to satisfy most people—and they would put up with the long wait.

I recommend that when you're in a prospect's office you want to set the stage so everything is working in your favor. This often means scheduling a meeting at a future date when the prospect can devote his or her undivided attention to what you have to sell.

I admit that it's tempting to give an on-the-spot presentation to an eager prospect who greets you warmly and announces: "Come right into my office and let me see what you've got to sell, but make it fast because I've got only twenty minutes and then I've got a board meeting."

Obviously, it is self-defeating to try to give a sixty-minute presentation in twenty minutes. In this situation, I advise you to look at your watch and say: "Mr. Prospect, I'm sorry, but I'm running late for an appointment, and as much as I'd like to, I don't have five minutes to spare. The sole purpose of my call today was to stop by to introduce myself. I only work by appointment, so let's set up a date when we can get together for an hour, which is the time I need to adequately present my product to you."

This straightforward approach demonstrates that you respect your prospect's time as much as your own. What's more, it provides you with a solid appointment with a bona fide prospect, and establishes you as a professional. Chances are good that the next time you walk into his office, his sales resistance will be down.

Naturally, the amount of time that a prospect grants to a salesperson depends on what is being sold. Obviously, an office supplies sales representative only requires a few minutes of time to sell a few boxes of pencils, copier paper, staples, and so on. On the other hand, an estate planning advisor might require several hours to make a presentation. And some require even more time than this. For instance, an initial meeting to present a complicated computer systems program could require a day-long meeting with several top company executives. And the first meeting is just the beginning of what may turn out to be hundreds of hours of meetings until the sale is finalized.

MOST SALESPEOPLE ARE NEGATIVE

It's true. The majority of salespeople don't expect to close a sale. They've had their brains knocked out so many times that they're actually surprised when they succeed.

It always amazed me how the other car salespeople at the dealership where I worked would huddle together in small bull sessions every morning. It's what I refer to as the "dope ring" for obvious reasons. I was a loner and kept to myself. Just like Ted Williams was a loner—and the last baseball player to hit .400.

When I'd arrive at work, I saw no purpose in wasting my time talking to them. After all, they weren't going to buy a car from me! Besides, I didn't get up that morning to shoot the bull. I didn't have time to hear any of their jokes, and I didn't spend my lunch hour with other car salespeople.

My business was to sell cars, and I didn't want to hear other salespeople griping all day. But I couldn't help overhearing them. Customers would walk into the showroom and a salesman would say: "You take that one, I don't want him. He's just a shopper." Another would eye the next customer and remark, "Oh, he's got his old lady with him. That's a bad sign." Somebody else would say, "Look at this mooch. He can't even afford to wear a decent coat." The next customer's hair was too long. And another belonged to an ethnic group that "don't buy cars." All day long those guys would think up reasons why people weren't good prospects. I couldn't get over it. It was as if they were trying to convince themselves that nobody ever bought cars. But me, I believed that every person who walked into the showroom was there for one reason: to buy a car! I figured every person who walked into the showroom had one thought in mind—he or she wanted to buy a car. Why else would anyone come into an automobile dealership?

To this day I could never figure out what those salespeople know that I don't know. How in the world can anyone look at somebody and determine if he's going to buy? I've been in the sales field for many years and I still have no idea what a buyer is supposed to look like, and I defy anyone to describe what one looks like.

The same negative thinking happens with outside salespeople. They spend the majority of their time driving past prospects, not even bothering to make the effort to get out of their cars to make the calls. They spend half of their time thinking up reasons why people won't buy instead of giving sales presentations.

Then, when they do work up the courage to make a sales presentation, they're full of doubts and fears. I can't stand being around negative people, and I can't help thinking prospects feel this way, too. After all, who needs some down-in-the-mouth guy walking into his or her place of business to cast a cloud of doom over the joint? What would you do if somebody like that came into your home or office? I'd resist him like the plague.

I always understood why people were so turned off by negative salespeople. Knowing this, I make a special effort to convince myself that everyone is a terrific prospect. I am so positive I'm going to make a sale that I can't help but generate enthusiasm from every prospect I meet. Believe me, it is contagious. Isn't this a refreshing contrast to those salespeople out there spreading negative thoughts wherever they go? And they can't figure out why they encounter so much resistance!

IT'S HARD TO SAY NO

After all I've told you about all that sales resistance out there, I don't think it will come as a shock to say there are many folks who feel apprehensive, troubled, and uneasy about those of us who sell for a living.

But then you can't blame them, if, in their minds, being sold is comparable to being pressured, harassed, and coerced into making a decision against one's will. Understandably, there's no enjoyment in being treated this way.

Let us remember that salespeople are motivated to influence others to make decisions, and to some people *any* decision-making doesn't go down too well. This is a subject I'll cover in detail in the chapter "Handling Objections." But in spite of all of the mistreatment and abuse people expect to receive, subconsciously there's still one other anxiety that constantly hangs over their heads when they encounter even a salesperson they like: *People don't like saying no.*

Take a moment to think about what I just said. Isn't it

infinitely easier to say yes than it is to say no? Every parent knows how much easier it is to give in to a child. And it's no easy task to say no to a persuasive salesperson you find charming and sincere. Sure, if the guy is a real s.o.b., you don't mind hurting his feelings by rejecting him, but your feelings are quite different toward the nice salesperson who's given you the royal treatment.

Think about when you've spent an hour or so listening to a considerate professional salesperson talk to you about the merits of owning his or her product. You were given some intelligent and logical reasons to buy, and you understood how much the salesperson wanted your business. Under these circumstances, most decent people experience a sense of guilt for having occupied the salesperson's time only to have him or her walk out empty-handed. After all, the salesperson works on a commission and, like the rest of us, has a family to support. See what I mean? People know that even when they encounter a low-pressure, "Mr. Nice Guy" salesperson, they'll be put on the spot and feel an obligation to make a buying decision. All of this adds up to mean that some degree of anxiety will always be present.

Because it is hard for people to say no, it may be harder to get your foot in their doors, but then, once you do, this works in your favor. This is especially true when there is a need for your product and you excel in presenting it. Couple this with sincerity and conviction—and those nos will become yeses.

2

SELLING YOURSELF

I've already told you that I have been recognized as the world's number one retail salesperson. However, because this chapter is titled "Selling Yourself," I'm telling it to you again. What I didn't mention before is that I also sell the world's number one product—ME! *I sell Joe Girard.*

At the risk of sounding egotistical, it wouldn't make any difference what I sold—automobiles, computers, real estate; I'd still sell the world's number one product. I'd feel this way if I were a CPA, an attorney, a doctor. No matter what I did for a living, I'd brainwash myself into thinking I was number one. If I didn't think this way, no one else would either.

And you should also believe that *you* sell the world's number one product—*YOU!*

"Say, Joe," I've been asked, "how could we both sell the world's number one product?"

The answer is, every one of us is unique. There's no one else in the world like me or like you.

I think it's vital for you to know that you're unique. Once you do, you'll realize how much of a difference you make in determining whether the prospect buys your product. Let's face it, we each have a monopoly on our own unique combination of attributes.

No matter what you sell, you make a difference. There are nearly 2,000 life insurance companies offering the same products; all stockbrokers selling listed securities have the same stocks and bonds to sell; real estate agents sell multiple-listed properties. The same is true in the office supply and equipment field, in the retail clothing business, in the supermarket industry, and so on.

What this all boils down to is, you must sell yourself. The prospect must like you and believe in you. If not, there is no reason anyone should buy from you instead of someone else.

SELL YOUR COMPANY

I'm not suggesting that you sell yourself so exclusively that you fail to sell your company. While I do believe that you're the more important of the two, the reputation of your company is a strong selling feature to help close sales.

It is particularly helpful in establishing credibility when making a cold call. While a prospect might not be familiar with you, he is certain to recognize the name of prominent companies such as IBM, Merrill Lynch, Prudential, General Electric, General Motors, and so on. Knowing that you are associated with a reputable firm helps erase doubts that the prospect might otherwise have about doing business with a stranger. By eliminating these suspicions, you have removed an objection that might have arisen at the close of the sale. The prospect is presold on knowing your company will stand behind its product. Then, too, the prospect knows that prestigious organizations hire top-quality people, so in a sense you're selling yourself when you sell the good name of your company.

It's a mistake not to sell your company's strong points. But some salespeople hesitate in doing so because they're insecure. They think that if they ever leave to represent a competitor, the customers will continue to do business with the original company. In reality, if you treat your customers properly, they'll follow you to the ends of the earth to do business with you. Stop and think about it. When you buy products such as investments or life insurance, isn't it true that your loyalties lie with the representative? As our society becomes more and more service-oriented, the salesperson's role becomes an even greater factor.

What if you represent a smaller or less-known company? Then you must concentrate on building a reputation of excellence on your own. If you already deal with an associate of your prospect, perhaps that associate can call the prospect with an introduction. If not, you must rely on your own strong points while pushing the attributes of your company. Who knows? Perhaps with your finesse and know-how, you can put your company on the map. In fact, I put my dealer on the map. At dealers' conventions, he'd draw crowds of people asking questions about me.

In fact, no matter what size firm you represent, the customer probably will have few if any contacts in the company with anyone but you. A stockbroker representing such firms as Merrill Lynch, Shearson Lehman Hutton, or Dean Witter is backed by a giant institution, but his clients have no personal contact with any other firm member except perhaps the telephone receptionist. The same is true when an individual buys insurance from Metropolitan, John Hancock, Paul Revere, or any other insurer. It is the agent who is the sole contact. In a sense, the salesperson *is* the company—the only human contact the customer ever has!

BEING SOLD ON WHAT YOU SELL

Before you can sell your product to somebody else, you must be 100 percent sold on it yourself. Otherwise, you can't sell with conviction, and no matter how much you try to fake it, people will see right through you.

Martin Shafiroff, acclaimed as one of the top retail stockbrokers in the world with Shearson Lehman Hutton, believes strongly in having conviction. He states: "All great business successes have strong convictions in what they are doing. Essentially, the first person you must sell to, if you want to succeed, is yourself. I believe this is vital. When you believe in what you are doing, the other party evaluating your comments is going to react accordingly. For this reason, I believe an individual must seek out, that is, study, review, and analyze the entire investment spectrum until he can come up with a product and a strategy for which he can develop strong convictions."[1]

Shafiroff feels that only when you have these strong convictions can you superimpose your beliefs onto others. He thinks that a salesperson's convictions are so powerful that even when he sells investments over the telephone, they can be felt by the other party thousands of miles away! The proof of the pudding is that Shafiroff has more clients who are presidents and board chairmen of Fortune 500 companies than any other broker, even though he has yet to meet 75 percent of them in person.

Conviction comes when salespeople believe so strongly in the value of their product that their single driving motivation is to provide value to their customers. The truly great salespeople in this world are more anxious to provide benefits to their customers than they are to receive large commissions. When money is the major driving force, salespeople rarely succeed. Prospects can see the dollar signs in a salesperson's eyes, and it's written all over their faces. You must think about the best interests of your customers. Your interests should be secondary. Forget about the money; those large commission checks will come automatically when you look out for your customers.

I sold Chevrolets, and sure, I knew that there were better cars being produced. I was fully aware that a Chevy didn't drive as well as a Mercedes or a BMW. But I firmly believed it was an excellent value for the money. And I knew that any prospect who worked within a certain budget would get his full money's worth. I had to believe this or I wouldn't have been able to sell Chevrolets.

You must believe your product is the best value of its kind. An excellent way to demonstrate it is by putting your money where your mouth is and *owning it*. I always drove a Chevy, yet I saw Chevrolet dealers drive to their showrooms in Caddies and Mercedes. Anytime I'd see them do that, I became a little sick in the stomach. Sure, I could have afforded to own any car, but by doing so, my customers would think: "Girard thinks he's too good to drive what he sells." To my way of thinking, that's a stupid message to convey.

No matter what you sell, you should own it yourself. Once when a life insurance agent was trying to sell me a $500,000 policy, I asked him how much he owned on his life. "Er, I'm insured for twenty-five thousand dollars, Joe," he said in a low voice. After that comment, no matter what he told me, I had no confidence in what he said. It didn't matter that he might have had a good product that I needed. Emotionally, I didn't feel comfortable with him. Several weeks later, I asked the same question of another life insurance agent who matter-of-factly replied, "I own a million-dollar policy." He said it with such conviction that I knew he believed in what he was attempting to sell me, and I bought a large policy from him.

There's a definite message—a negative one—that people send when they fail to use their own products, which put food on their tables. I remember reading an article in *Fortune* magazine titled "How I Would Turn Around GM," by the outspoken Ross Perot.[2] He opposed top managers being chauffeur-driven to work. Perot declared that "anyone who needed a chauffeur to drive him to work was probably too old to be on the payroll, and that anybody in a car company ought to be driving his own car because you didn't get much of a feel for how the car handles in the backseat. We shouldn't be giving handmade cars to executives." Perot's point is right on target. When you don't use the product you sell, you're signaling: "It's okay for you to use what I sell, but it isn't good enough for me." Now that's a helluva thing to tell customers!

Demonstrating your belief in what you sell is basic and is applicable to every product, not just automobiles. Imagine going into a fine men's clothing store and having a sales clerk wait on you who is dressed in a cheap suit. Or having a woman behind the cosmetics counter who isn't wearing makeup. Or a slightly obese representative from a physical fitness center trying to sell you a lifetime membership.

POSITIVE THINKING MUST BE REALISTIC THINKING

I don't intend to get into a lengthy talk about the powers of positive thinking, a subject on which my good friend Norman

Vincent Peale wrote several books. But I don't think a book on how to close sales could be complete without a few words about the significance of having a positive mental attitude. For the record, I don't recall ever meeting a successful person in any field who was a negative thinker. Positive thinking is the single common denominator to all successful people.

To be a successful salesperson, you must believe that you will sell to every prospect. I am not suggesting, however, that simply by thinking about closing sales you will make it happen automatically. A salesperson who has no product knowledge, sales experience, or training, but who thinks he can sell every prospect, is a wishful thinker, not a positive thinker. You can't simply wake up in the morning, look in the mirror, and expect to see a successful salesperson staring back at you. You must earn the right to have a strong self-image; otherwise, you will deceive only yourself.

VISUALIZING

In biofeedback, a patient is hooked up to a device that feeds back information on his physiological processes, which are monitored. For example, somebody with tachycardia, a rapid heartbeat, can be hooked up to a oscilloscope to obtain a constant readout of the heartbeat. Then the patient is instructed to relax and watch the monitor. Next he is told to form a mental picture of something peaceful and serene, such as sitting on the beach, watching the waves roll in. "Feel the warm sun and feel the ocean breeze," he is advised. The more the patient relaxes, the more real his image picture becomes. As a result of this mental exercise, a visual display shows that the patient's heartbeat actually is slowing down. Most interesting is that the biofeedback instrument did nothing but record what happened as a result of the patient's thinking!

Stephanie Simonton, a world-renowned psychotherapist, specializes in working with cancer patients. By telling them how to do imagery exercises, Simonton teaches patients to visualize healthy white cells attacking and destroying cancer cells. Incredibly, some patients have been able to realize a drop in the number of cancer cells through this mental exercise. This, coupled with medical treatment, can curtail the spread of cancer and even cure it. If visualization can help defeat a dreaded disease such as cancer, imagine how it can help you develop and improve your selling skills.

The method is nothing new. One of the greatest heavyweight boxers, Gentleman Jim Corbett, used this technique in preparing for his title fight in 1892 with John L. Sullivan, who had been the world champion for ten years. Corbett practiced his left jab by shadowboxing, throwing tens of thousands of punches at his own image in a mirror. Going into the ring as a heavy underdog, Corbett credits this training method with his capturing the championship title in what is viewed as one of the major events in boxing history.

Muhammad Ali is another former world heavyweight champion who used visualization, although early in his career the public didn't know what to make of it. Announcing to one and all in person, in the locker room, in the ring, in front of TV cameras, and during all media interviews, Ali boasted that he was *the greatest!* In the beginning, the public laughed when he'd recite what many called childlike poetry: "I'm gonna float like a butterfly / And sting like a bee / I'm gonna knock him out in five / And he ain't ever gonna be alive." After Ali won the championship, people stopped laughing at him. Muhammad Ali became one of the best heavyweight boxers in the history of the sport.

If visualization is powerful enough to destroy cancer cells and to knock out heavyweight champions, it must certainly have some merit. Just as an athlete forms mental pictures of a great performance (swinging a golf club, shooting a basketball, kicking field goals, etc.), you can picture yourself closing sales. Take yourself through an entire sales presentation while driving to your next call, or if you're an indoor salesperson, on your way to work. Visualize your customer's gratitude for the fine service you'll give him, and be sure to picture him signing an order form and handing a check to you as a down payment.

What you visualize eventually becomes reality. When you believe you're going to close every sale, you'll discover that your percentage of successful closes will dramatically increase.

I've run into a lot of doubting Thomases who don't buy what I tell them about visualization. "That's daydreaming, Joe. I've got better things to do with my time," they say.

These are the same guys in the "dope rings" who knock every prospect who walks into the showroom to buy a car. They don't even want to *think* about selling anyone.

A WINNING SELF-IMAGE

Former first lady Eleanor Roosevelt once said: "No one can make you feel inferior without your consent." I fully agree that if you see yourself as inferior, this is how you will come across to others. I think this is particularly true in the field of selling.

Shafiroff, who, as a stockbroker, sells almost exclusively on the telephone, believes that one's self-image is a major factor, contrary to what many people would think, *particularly* during a telephone sales presentation. He claims to have witnessed salespeople trained to deliver identical telephone presentations, and over a period of time the ones with a winning self-image outproduced those with poor self-images. "It's how each individual perceives himself that counts," Shafiroff explains. "If you think of yourself as a very important person, the other guy will see you as a VIP, too."[3]

He points out that many top salespeople speak with accents, mispronounce words, have gravel voices, and so on. Even so, those with good self-images constantly outsell those with low self-esteem. "By and large, your sense of your own importance will determine whether your telephone prospect develops a positive image of you," Shafiroff tells. "In person, you might come across as a VIP by wearing an expensive suit and having a distinguished profile. But on the telephone, a prospect does not have an opportunity to see you. He must form a mental picture based on how you come across. *He will tend to see you as you see yourself.* And very often the image he forms will not look a bit like you! How many times, for example, have you met someone in person after knowing him only over the telephone? When that happens, you often are startled. The individual is very different from what you imagined. He may be older or taller or heavier. He may dress differently from what you thought he would. When this happens, you tend to think the telephone image was 'wrong.' But perhaps what we *see* is merely a facade, and the telephone image is the real thing—a more accurate representation of what the person is really like. As we know, appearances can be deceiving."

Shafiroff makes a strong point. However, I believe that a salesperson's self-image also is visible in his or her body language and facial expressions, which cannot be communicated during a telephone conversation. For instance, an individual with a poor self-image will drag himself into a prospect's office. You've seen this character before—the Willy Loman–type salesperson from playwright Arthur Miller's *Death of a Salesman*. But the salesperson full of vim and vigor struts in with a spring to his step—the Professor Harold Hill–type from *The Music Man*. Each one's self-image signals either positive or negative vibes. Just how you feel about yourself is telegraphed by the way you talk, stand, and walk. And you do it by the way you smile and frown. Believe me, although you might not think you're conveying signals to your prospects, you are. It's written all over your face.

When business is slow and you're feeling down, I recommend calling several of your satisfied customers for a brief chat. But make the call serve a dual purpose. Perhaps you can pass on some new information that will benefit them or simply inquire how they feel about the quality of service they're receiving. Then let them talk—and listen. Hearing their good thoughts about your product and service will reinforce your belief in what you sell and generate positive thoughts for your self-image. As an added benefit, you may pick up a reorder and some referrals. There's nothing like making a sale to boost your self-image when you're in a slump.

BE PREPARED!

"Be prepared" is more than a motto for the Boy Scouts. These words should be tattooed on the chest of every salesperson so he or she will remember it. For starters, entering a sales presentation fully prepared does wonders for your self-confidence. Knowing that you know everything about your product, company, and competition, backward and forward, works miracles in elevating your self-image. Then, too, nothing beats doing your homework so you know exactly what your prospect's problems are—and have solutions for them. It's a great feeling to know that no fastball can be thrown to dust you off. The only way to be assured of this kind of comfort is by doing your homework in advance so you're 100 percent certain you can handle any situation that might arise.

A top residential real estate agent, for instance, will spend a major portion of her day researching homes. She will spend hours looking at multiple-listed homes prior to showing them to a client to learn everything about it. After her research, the agent can tell her client about every feature, including who the builder was, when it was built, the financing, the taxes, and so on.

John W. Galbreath, one of the nation's largest real estate developers, also feels strongly about preparedness. His son, Dan, now heads John W. Galbreath & Co., and the senior Galbreath takes great delight in telling how Dan once prepared himself for an important sales presentation: "I kept hammering the importance of being prepared into Dan when he first came into our business, and fortunately, he got the message right away. Dan and I were negotiating a deal with the president of a large corporation that involved our developing a six-million-dollar building on a lease-back arrangement. With a deal of this nature, you must be exact with the interest rates and the amount of rent you're talking about. One decimal-point fluctuation in the interest rate can have a tremendous dollar effect on rent over ten or twenty years. So prior to the meeting with the company, I suggested to Dan that he memorize the rent tables covering the spread between 3.5 and 5.5 percent interest.

"And don't you know it, as we got into the last stages of negotiating, the corporation's president asked us to calculate several different rent figures based on different interest rates. He must have expected us to ask to borrow his calculator, but instead, Dan started rattling off the figures on the different rents figured at the various interest rates. Naturally, the president realized that Dan had done his homework before sitting down at the meeting. Certainly he knew that nobody could calculate interest rates that fast in his head. But he was obviously impressed that Dan had come to the meeting well prepared. Dan had won his respect, and he had confidence in us—enough so that we got the job."[4]

Galbreath insists, "You've got to be prepared. That's the basis for all of it. You just have to know more about your business, and there's nothing more disrespectful or presumptuous than going into another person's office and not being able to make it worth his time. If you're not able to answer all of his questions, then you've wasted his time—and your own. You owe him an apology."[5]

Not only is it rude to walk into somebody's office unprepared, but when you do, you're likely to have feelings of distraction, anxiety, and guilt. Consequently, you lose the sense of being in charge, which, for obvious reasons, is self-defeating.

As you can see, I'm a strong believer in doing what you have to do to believe in yourself. But being fully prepared goes beyond this. It's practical. You must have the knowledge and ability to pass on certain information to your prospect so he or she can make an intelligent buying decision. If a prospect doesn't know specific reasons why he should buy your product, he simply won't recognize why it is of value to him. For example, he might not realize why your product is a better buy than your competitor's unless you know what XYZ Company is offering so you can emphasize the differences. So not only must you do your homework to thoroughly know your product, you must be able to make comparisons to what your competition offers. For instance, a prospect might say: "A salesperson from XYZ Company left me a proposal, and I think they've got you beat."

By knowing the strengths and weaknesses of XYZ's product, you can emphasize a unique selling point that you exclusively offer, and this difference can win the sale. But if you aren't aware of what is different, you leave it to chance that you will come up with a need that will convince the prospect to buy.

As a salesperson, you should take the same approach to your career as do professionals in other fields such as accounting, law, and medicine. The only way these professional people can keep current with the vast changes that are constantly taking place in their professions is to spend several hours each week reading published materials, having discussions with their peers, and regularly attending seminars. While I don't advocate engaging in bull sessions that are nonproductive, I do believe in exchanging ideas with the top professionals in your field. I strongly recommend that you become an expert in your field—there's no excuse to settle for being anything less, even if it means spending an extra hour or two reading several times a week. As a professional salesperson, you must do your homework.

THE APPEARANCE OF SUCCESS

While we're constantly told not to judge a book by its cover, we do. We're all influenced by things as they appear to be on the surface. If this were not true, the publishing industry would stop spending millions of dollars in the multicolor book jacket designs every year. Or for that matter, neither would the packagers of grocery products sell their merchandise today in designer boxes and bottles. In fact, the cost of the package is often more than its contents. I'm sure everybody knows the value in selling goods by sprucing up their appearance, and likewise, your appearance makes a major difference in selling you.

I recall car salesmen wearing loud outfits, appearing as if they were on their way to the racetrack after work. They wore fancy jewelry that included gold chains and pinky rings. In short, they were dressed like the stereotyped fast-talking salesman and gave the impression you could trust them just about as far as you could throw them. To make matters worse, they wore sunglasses, day and night, summer, autumn, winter, and spring. Now don't get me wrong. The kind of clothes people wear is not actually a factor in determining their honesty. But we're talking about dressing for success, and if you present yourself as what people perceive as a fly-by-night salesman, you can be sure some people will be turned off.

A good rule of thumb on how to dress properly is: When in

doubt, dress conservatively. Unless, of course, you happen to sell a line of high-fashion clothing, in which case you should wear what you sell. I recommend that no matter how much you personally enjoy wearing outrageous outfits, save them for your nonworking hours. It is not worth losing business because you look unprofessional.

Recently, an attractive saleswoman called on me to sell me some tax-shelter investments. She was dressed beautifully—that is, if she were going to a formal dinner party. She wore a low-cut dress, and frankly, I was distracted by her partially exposed bosom and she made me feel uncomfortable. Now I'm by no means prudish. It simply was hard for me to concentrate on her sales presentation because she was dressed so inappropriately. It reminded me of what famed fashion designer Coco Chanel said, that if a woman is dressed poorly, you notice her dress, and if she's impeccably dressed, you notice the woman. However, in this instance, I must admit I noticed more than her dress.

Then, too, when the buyer recognizes what is an obvious violation of the acceptable dress code within your industry, it makes him think: "If this salesperson doesn't have the good sense to know how to dress properly, how good is his judgment? I don't want his advice on how to handle my business affairs."

The appearance of success goes much further than the clothes you wear, the cosmetics you use, and the way you do your hair. Your image is even projected by the car you drive, including the model, year, and condition in which you keep it. For instance, a real estate broker's car serves as his or her mobile office. Prospects are transported to and from properties in it, during which time business is discussed. An old beat-up car sends a message that the broker cannot afford a decent automobile. Likewise, an unkempt car filled with fast-food wrappings, work papers, and cigarette butts indicates disorganization. These are not the signals that you want your prospect to receive.

For the same obvious reasons, the appearance of your office makes a difference. Say, for instance, that you're shopping around for homeowner's insurance, and you visit two offices representing the same insurer. One agency has a plush office, furnished with all the trimmings of success, in a suburban high-rise office building. The other, located in a blighted neighborhood, looks as if it has been struck by a tornado. Which would you most likely choose to handle your insurance? Keep in mind that both agencies have identical policies with the same prices. As you can see, rightly or wrongly, people's confidence level is strongly influenced by appearances. Their mental gymnastics is: "If this guy can't afford a decent office (car, suit, etc.), he must not be successful." It is true that most people make appearances of success and failure decisive factors in determining one's capacity to provide good service.

THE INVISIBLE SIGN—
"MAKE ME FEEL IMPORTANT!"

In her best-seller, *Mary Kay on People Management*, Mary Kay Ash, founder of Mary Kay Cosmetics, says: "Every person is special! I sincerely believe this. Each of us wants to feel good about himself or herself, but to me it is just as important to make others feel the same way. Whenever I meet someone, I try to imagine him wearing an invisible sign that says: MAKE ME FEEL IMPORTANT! I respond to this sign immediately, and it works wonders."[6]

It's no wonder that Mary Kay Ash is one of the most successful businesswomen in the history of America. She knows how to sell herself by making other people feel important.

I think it's a matter of showing people that you're sincerely interested in them. For instance, when a customer walks in covered with dirt and wearing a hard hat, I say: "Mmm, you must be in the construction business." Now, everybody likes to talk about himself and I try to open him up.

"That's right," he replies.

"What are you in? Steel? Concrete?" I ask to get a conversation going.

I remember asking one guy what his business was and he replied: "I work at a screw machine shop."

"No kidding. What do you do all day?"

"I make screws."

"Really. I can't picture how they make screws. You know, I'd like to come down to your place one day and see how you do it. Would that be okay?"

See what I was doing? I was showing him that I cared about him. Probably nobody ever asked him what he does with so much interest. Instead, a typical car salesman might joke, "You make screws—you gotta be screwed up."

During my slow time, I'd make it a point to go to his shop and visit him. You can't believe how happy he'd be to see me. He would introduce me to his fellow workers and proudly say, "This is the guy I bought my car from." I gave everyone my business card, and I picked up a lot of extra business this way. And as a bonus, I got to see a lot of fascinating things that helped me relate to my customers—to speak their language.

From the moment a customer of mine walks into the dealership, I don't care if I haven't seen him for five years, I make him feel as if I saw him yesterday, and I really missed him.

"Say, where have you been, Bill?" I say with a warm smile.

"Er, well, I haven't needed a car up until now," he apologizes.

"Do you have to need a car just to stop in and say hello when you're passing by? I thought we were friends."

"W-well, we are, Joe."

"You pass by our showroom every day going back and forth to work, Bill. From now on I want you to stop in once in a while and say hello. Now come on in my office and tell me what you've been up to."

How many times have you walked out of a restaurant and said to the person with you, "Remind me never to go back there again, will you?" Do you know what builds great restaurants? They're built by word of mouth, because people tell other people how much the management cared for you. The great restaurants in this country have love and care coming out of their kitchens. They have people in the kitchen who are looking out to make sure that the person in the dining room is going to get a fair shake and a fair deal—and a good meal.

I want my customers to leave with the same feeling that people get when they walk out of a great restaurant. You know, that satisfied, contented feeling.

I remember a middle-aged woman who once came into the

showroom saying that she wanted to kill some time and look at some cars. She said that her heart was set on buying a Ford, but the salesman down the street told her to come back in an hour. She told me that her mind was made up and she wanted a white Ford coupe, one just like her sister-in-law's. The woman said, "It's a present to myself in honor of my birthday. I'm fifty-five years old today."

"Happy birthday," I said, and I excused myself, saying I'd be back in a minute. When I came back, I said, "As long as you have some time on your hands, let me show you one of our coupes—it, too, comes in white."

About fifteen minutes later, one of the office girls walked in and handed me a dozen roses. "These aren't for me," I said. "It's not my birthday." With that, I gave them to the woman. "And many happy returns of the day," I said.

She was so touched, her eyes began to water. "I haven't had anyone give me flowers in ages," she said.

As we talked, she told me about the Ford she wanted. "But the salesman wasn't very nice. I suppose he saw me drive up in my old car and assumed I couldn't afford to buy a new model. In the middle of showing me some cars, one of the other salesmen shouted over that he was going out to grab a bite and asked if he could bring anything back. With that, the salesman waiting on me said, 'Wait. I'll go with you.' So that's why I had some time to kill."

I'm sure you've guessed that she didn't buy a Ford. She bought a Chevy from me and wrote a check for the entire amount. This story tells you something, doesn't it? When you make a customer feel important, he or she is even willing to buy his or her second choice.

SELLING ON YOUR OWN TURF

If given a choice, remember that the home team has an enormous advantage in sports. The same is true in selling. So don't hesitate to invite your customers to your office if this is an option. Of course, if your office is so run-down that it's a source of embarrassment to you, then that's a horse of a different color.

First, you're bound to exercise more control in your own office—if for no other reason than you can dictate what interruptions, if any, are permissible. In a customer's office, you have no say in keeping secretaries or other employees from coming and going as they choose, or as the prospect chooses. And of course you can't order the switchboard not to put any calls through, but you can on your own turf.

Second, as Mark McCormack, who founded and heads IMG (International Management Group), the worldwide sports agency, explains, "A meeting on your own turf brings with it a sense of 'invasion' by the other party. There is a tension there, however sublimated (subconscious) it may be. Simply by being polite and making the other person feel comfortable you can diffuse that tension and earn a certain amount of confidence and trust even before the meeting begins."[7]

Third, you can take advantage of some good "props" that are otherwise unavailable in somebody else's office. For instance, I believe in using office walls as valuable space to make a statement. I like to think of my office walls as free billboard space. They can say good things about me that would sound egotistical for me to say about myself. So it's a subtle way to get the message to my customers. For instance, my walls had plaques that were awarded to me for my sales records, and there were also framed pictures of newspaper and magazine articles, photographs taken of me with some VIPs, and so on. I even had a photo of former president Gerald Ford and me on my wall. These billboards help to sell Joe Girard.

Note that I don't have anything on my walls to confuse my customers. There are no photographs of cars because I don't want a prospect to think about any other model except the one that I'm selling him. Nor is my desk cluttered with anything that might be distracting. And I sure didn't have anything in my offices that involved politics or religion. One of the salesmen at the dealership had a picture of the pope on his wall. I told him a million times, "Not everybody is Catholic, so that picture doesn't win any points for you with non-Catholics." Do you know what he told me when I said that? "That's their problem. Let 'em take their business somewhere else if they got anything against Catholics." There is one thing that I do keep on my desk, however, and I insist that every salesperson should do the same. *I keep an order pad on my desk*. I don't believe in keeping the main reason why the prospect is in my office some great big secret. I like everyone to know that I take orders in my office, and that order pad is always there to remind my customers that I do.

A real estate broker should do the same thing. In the residential field, in most communities, there's a standard printed real estate purchase contract that is approved by the local board of realtors that should be highly visible during any discussions between the buyer and broker. For instance, a prospect might say: "If the buyer would accept a contract for $400,000 with a contingency that I could have an architectural inspection, I'd put in an offer."

"Well, he's asking $450,000, but it doesn't hurt to come in at $400,000," the broker says as he writes the figure of $400,000 in the contract. "I'm also going to request that he gives you ten days after acceptance of the contract to have the inspection."

It's just like when they roll the patient into the operating room for surgery. All of the surgeon's tools are neatly arranged. It's no secret why the patient is there. Likewise, when I start using the order pad when it's time to close the sale, it doesn't come as a shock to my prospect.

One thing I don't believe in having on my desk is scratch pads. Yet I've observed many salespeople routinely using them to casually jot down notes about the prospect's comments. Car salespeople, for instance, write down details about what options their prospects mention they would like to have on an automobile. But when you put information on a memo pad, it later becomes awkward to transfer it to the order sheet. It causes a pause in your presentation when it's time to close the sale— exactly at the point when you don't want the prospect to say: "Hey, whatcha doin'? I didn't say to fill out that order sheet."

The trick is to take notes directly on the order sheet, explaining to the customer, if asked, that you're just trying to keep track of the desired features. Then when you're ready to close, all you need is a signature because the order sheet is already filled out!

HAVING A SENSE OF HUMOR

It's hard for me to imagine anyone who doesn't have a sense of humor. So, assuming that you have one, I think putting some comedy and lightness into your sales presentation is an appropriate way to sell yourself. It also is a nice touch that keeps the nature of your business more interesting. If nothing else, it helps to keep prospects alert—I actually fell asleep one night listening to a boring insurance agent trying to sell me a homeowner's policy! Needless to say, sleeping prospects don't buy anything!

When I suggest to you that humor is important, I am not advocating that you approach a prospect with a slap on the back and say, "Hey, ol' buddy, did you hear the one about the traveling saleslady?" If you do tell a joke, keep it clean and avoid ethnic jokes. I'm not against jokes, but there is a time and a place for everything.

Personally, I find that injecting humor at the right time is an excellent way to relax people. It makes them feel more comfortable and can sometimes break the ice during a tense moment. For example, when I ask somebody to sign an order form, and he just sits there unable to make up his mind, I'll say, "What's the matter, you got arthritis or something?" This usually gets a chuckle out of the prospect, and he'll break into a smile. I'll even put a pen in his hand and guide it to the order sheet and say, "Go on, put your John Hancock down." Naturally, I have a big grin on my face when I do it, but at the same time, I'm serious and he knows I'm serious. But it works because it makes people laugh, and then they sign their names on the dotted line.

If the prospect still can't make up his mind, I'll say, "What do I have to do to get your business? Do you want me to get down on my hands and knees and beg?" Then I'll actually get down on my knees, look up and say, "Okay, I'm begging you for your business. Now who can say no to a grown man who's on his knees? Now c'mon, will ya, sign your name." If this doesn't move him, I say, "What do you want me to do now? Do you want me to lie on my back? Okay, I'll lie down on my back."

This routine cracks most people up and they say, "Joe, *please* don't lie down on your back. Where do you want me to sign?" And then we both laugh—and he signs his name.

Sometimes, I take it one step further. "Do you know what, Frank? I hope you get a lemon." I give him a serious look and keep quiet.

"What do you mean," he asks, "you hope I get a lemon?"

"I really mean it. I hope you get a lemon so I can show off. Because I will give you so much service that I'll turn that lemon into a peach, and then I will own you for the rest of your life."

Sure I put on a good performance when I sell, and I'll tell you something else—my customers have a good time buying a car from me. I hear people say how much they dread going out to buy a car. Not my customers. It's not idle words when I tell them to "enjoy the experience of doing business with Joe Girard."

A word of caution: Don't use the arthritis line if you're trying to sell to an older person. If you offend people, you'll lose them forever. Use discretion. If you are selling orthopedic equipment or a prosthesis, don't tell the customer that you hope he or she gets a lemon. And please don't use morbid humor if you're trying to sell a life insurance policy.

Use some sensitivity in evaluating your product and each individual customer before you take off with humor that could possibly offend someone. On some people, it just won't work. If you are working with a banker, for example, chances are good that he or she will want to stick to the matter at hand because the deal is serious and should be treated as such. And if the banker gets the feeling that you don't take him or her seriously, how can you treat the business seriously? So use humor, but use it wisely, cautiously, and with good taste.

GIFTS OF OBLIGATION

I used to make it a ritual with everyone who came into my office to give him a round button with an apple on it that says: "I Like You." I also passed out heart-shaped balloons to people that said, "You'll Love a Joe Girard Deal."

People like it when other people are nice to their children, so I'd get down on my hands and knees and say to the kids, "Hi, what's your name? Hi, Johnny. Gee, you've sure got a nice kid. What a little cutie pie." Then, while I was still on my knees, I'd crawl over to my cabinet with Johnny, with his parents watching. "Johnny, I've got something for you. Wait until you see what I've got." And I'd reach into my cabinet and pull out a fistful of suckers. Then, still on my knees, I'd walk over to the customer's wife and say, "Now, Johnny, you take this one, and here, Mommy, you take the rest. And here are some balloons, Daddy. Johnny, Daddy will hold these for you. Now you be a good boy while I'm talking to your mommy and daddy." All this time, I'd still be on my knees. These were gifts of obligation, and part of the tools of selling. Now, how could anyone say no to somebody who's on his hands and knees with his or her kid?

A prospect might hit his pocket looking for cigarettes and say, "I thought I had some cigarettes."

"Just a minute," I'd say, and I'd pull out ten different brands from my cabinet. "What kind do you smoke?"

"Marlboro."

"Here you are," and I'd open the pack for him. I would then light a match for him and put the pack into his pocket. I put the match box with my name on it in his pocket, too.

"Gee, thanks, Joe. How much do I owe you?"

"Don't be silly," I'd reply.

What was I doing? *I was obligating him to me!*

My gifts of obligation were minor compared to the grand scale of those of some business people. For example, I've seen some high-powered executives spend a few grand for tickets to the Super Bowl or to a championship boxing match! Perhaps the best people in making their customers feel obligated are the casino-hotels in Las Vegas where they "comp" (a complimentary gift) the big rollers with round-trip first-class airline tickets, deluxe suites, gourmet meals, you name it, whatever the customer wants, the customer gets. These people have it down to a science, and they're masters of psychology. They make the guy feel like such a VIP that he feels obligated to live up to his role as "Mr. Big." He demonstrates his importance by rolling the dice with stacks of $100 chips, and the gambling houses get their money back many times over again.

Generally, gifts of obligation should be relatively inexpensive or else they can backfire by being viewed as a kickback. The last thing you want to do is offend customers and have them think you're trying to buy their business. Some companies are so sensitive about this that their buyers aren't even permitted to accept lunch from a salesperson. So be sure to do your homework in advance and be certain about what's acceptable and what isn't with your customers. Then, too, if you give expensive presents to customers, they may request that in lieu of the gift, they prefer to have you charge them a lower price.

SINCERITY

It should go without saying that you must come across with sincerity. And if you don't you're in for a difficult time.

I think being sincere is the easiest part of selling. It's simply a matter of caring about your customer and believing in what you sell. If you don't feel this way, my advice to you is to seek other employment or find a product to sell that you believe in.

It's imperative that sincerity be honest. Don't ever think about lying because once you lie, you've lost all credibility. And as far as I'm concerned, you're through. Finished. As the Greek writer of fables Aesop once said, "A liar will not be believed, even when he speaks the truth."

Another thing—don't make any promises that you can't keep. If it takes three months for your computer systems to be installed, don't say the company will do it in four weeks just to make the sale. Unkept promises will come back to haunt you later on. Be up-front with your customers, otherwise, those broken promises will kill your chances of generating repeat business and referrals.

I used to go a step further and tell my customers that it might take even longer than it actually would for the delivery of a car that wasn't in inventory. I did this because I knew that most people are like kids, and try to tell a child that Christmas has been postponed for several days! Of course, when the car came in a few days earlier, I was a big hero—and most importantly, the customer knew that what Joe Girard promises—he delivers!

There's more to being sincere than just being honest. Even honest people can be guilty of false flattery. And while it's fine to compliment people, undue praise will backfire because your target will see right through you. If that happens, he or she won't believe what you say during any of your sales presentation. After all, you've already established yourself as a phony. Don't think for a minute that people will believe any flattery you dish up. People are a lot smarter than some salespeople give them credit for. Potential customers will not be influenced by contrived or deceptive flattery. And remember, customers may be skeptical of you in the first place, so you shouldn't give them any reason to reinforce their doubts. Don't forget that your number one mission is to sell your product. Your prospect's time is valuable, and he's not interested in phony compliments. He wants to get down to business and find out what you can do for him.

Although I've already emphasized that being prepared is important, sometimes even the most professional salesperson can't have all the answers. If a prospect asks a question you can't answer, simply say: "I am sorry, but I can't answer that for you. But I will find out as soon as I get back to my office, and I'll call you immediately." Keep in mind that if you hear yourself saying this too often, then you are not properly prepared. But every now and then, such a statement demonstrates your sincerity. And it's far better than trying to bluff by giving the customer the wrong information. That can come back to haunt you.

Of course, if it's possible to find out the answer at the time of the question, then do so. For instance, if a customer asked me to explain the gear ratio of the car, I'd say, "Let's go find out from an expert." And I'd take him to our auto mechanic to hear it right from the horse's mouth.

Here are two good tips on how to generate sincerity visually: First, never wear sunglasses. Frankly, I don't care if you're selling land in the middle of the desert—you must establish eye contact with people, and sunglasses make this impossible.

Second, look people squarely in the eye when you speak to them, and when you listen, look at their lips. When somebody doesn't make eye contact like this, it is often interpreted as a sign of dishonesty. Personally, I've known a lot of honest people who simply were too shy to look me in the eye, but prospects don't believe a salesperson can be shy, so I urge you to make the effort to make eye contact, no matter how tough it might be.

I also believe that you must give every prospect your complete and undivided attention during a sales presentation. I don't think there's anything more offensive than to be in the company of somebody who's looking around the room when I'm speaking. Have you ever been in a restaurant with somebody who is constantly looking around the room while you're talking? I've seen salespeople give the once-over to a pretty waitress, a good-looking secretary, or even a prospect's attractive wife and daughter. Not only is this in poor taste, but it's signaling to the potential customer that you aren't really interested in him.

When you're talking to a client but not giving him your complete, undivided attention, he is thinking: "Who does this guy think he is? Unless he pays attention to me, I don't care what he's selling—even if he's giving it away—I don't want it." Remember that you don't just communicate verbally, but through your eyes, facial expressions, and body language. You must be totally sincere, and if you're not, he'll know it by your nonverbal communication. You can't fake it. Unless you act in his best interests, you'll come across as a fly-by-night.

It's also important to realize that sincere people aren't greedy. Don't make such a profitable deal for yourself that your prospect won't want to do business with you again. When I sold cars, I was always careful not to make so much money on a sale that the customer could later find out that he would have saved more somewhere else. That could ruin my reputation, and I definitely would lose the customer's future business. I wasn't out to sell him one car. I was after long-term, repeat business. A business deal is only a good deal when *both* parties feel it is.

All it takes to ruin your promising reputation is for one person to feel cheated. That person will tell another, who will tell another. The loss of one sale doesn't represent just one lost customer. Believe me, word gets around. The small amount of additional profit you'll make by working yourself a better deal in one transaction will never compensate for all the money you'll lose by sending future potential customers to the competition. You give one person a good deal, and the effects will snowball quickly. And your wallet and reputation will expand accordingly.

3
ASSUMING THE SALE

Assuming the sale is so basic that my first reaction is to presume that you already understand the concept. But you probably don't know enough to make a significant difference. So, no matter how much you *think* you know, I want you to read this chapter thoroughly.

Everywhere you turn, you're exposed to other people assuming the sale. When the service station attendant asks, "Fill 'er up?" he's assuming not only that you've decided to buy gasoline, but also that you want as much as your tank will hold. Several years ago, Gulf Oil service station attendants were trained to ask: "Fill it up with No-Nox?" Not only did they assume the customer wanted a full tank, but they also assumed the customer wanted the highest-priced, top-of-the-line, premium gasoline!

You may be thinking that when a car pulls up next to the gasoline pumps, any fool could figure out that the driver is there to buy some gas. And when a customer walks into a fast food restaurant, you know he or she must be hungry.

It doesn't matter what you sell, the people walk through your doors because they are interested in your product. If they weren't, they wouldn't come in. I'll take it even one step further. You can make the same assumption about people who listen to salespeople who call on them at their homes and offices. It doesn't make a whole lot of sense for them to listen if they have no interest. And believe me, few people listen just to be polite. If they don't want to hear your sales presentation, they're not shy about telling you to hit the road!

People are always asking me: "When do you start to assume the sale, Joe?"

"Anytime I'm in front of a warm body that will hear me out," I reply.

"If that's true, Joe, then you assume every customer is going to buy. . ."

"You got it," I tell them.

I even assume the people who give me the most initial resistance will become some of my prime prospects. I figure that these people *know* they don't have any sales resistance, and once you give them a presentation, they *know* they're going to buy. Therefore, they put up a fierce fight to avoid salespeople. For this reason, I'm confident that once I get into my presentation they can't say no, and I have an easy sale.

One top life insurance agent told me that he assumes the sale even when a prospect doesn't keep an appointment. "I call back the following evening," the agent tells, "and I apologize because '*I* wasn't able to make it last night.' Of course, I was there on time, but neither he nor anyone else answered his door, so he doesn't know that. If he was hiding and wouldn't answer the door, he sure as hell doesn't want to tell me that. I figure that if he doesn't have the nerve to tell me he was the one who broke the appointment, I know he doesn't have any sales resistance, and I've got a sure thing once I pitch him."

ASSUME, ASSUME, ASSUME

No matter how repetitious it seems, throughout every presentation I keep assuming the sale. And you should, too. It should be built right into your presentation. Start doing it from the very beginning and keep right on doing it until the sale is closed. As far as I'm concerned, you can't assume the sale too much.

Contrary to what many novice salespeople think, you don't start assuming the sale only after reaching the point when you ask for the order. Everything you do is done with the thought in mind that your prospect is going to buy your product. You continually assume the sale—over and over—and before your prospect knows it, he starts to assume that he or she is going to buy, too.

Some people call it brainwashing. That's okay. Let them. Frankly, I don't think there's anything wrong with a little brainwashing if that's what it takes to convince people to buy what's good for them. A good analogy is subliminal advertising. This is where a commercial on television or in a movie theater relays a message to you that registers only in your subconscious mind. The message is placed on one frame in every so many, and it happens so quickly that you don't see it with the naked eye. But your subconscious mind picks it up and it registers the thought! A while back, a subliminal advertising experiment was conducted in a movie house. The audience was shown a subliminal message that said: "You are thirsty, you are thirsty." Within minutes, people were standing in long lines at the concession counters to purchase soft drinks. When you continually assume the sale, you're doing the same thing. You're relaying a signal to the prospect's subconscious that he or she will buy your product. His or her subconscious mind is picking up the message "Buy, buy."

I'm sure that if you're like me, there have been occasions when you've walked into a store to shop around with no intention of buying anything. Many times I'll have an hour or so to spare between flights, so I'll walk into the airport men's store to pass some time and to see the latest fashions. I can't tell you how many times I've bought clothes when I was only shopping around. I walk out shaking my head and talking to myself: "What in the world made me buy all this stuff? I have a wardrobe big enough to clothe a small army!" Then, about 15,000 feet in the air, I sit back and a big grin spreads across my face. The guy next to me thinks I've gone bananas when I say out loud: "That ol' son of a gun. Why, he kept right on assuming I was going to buy something, and I sure did!" Then I get a good chuckle out of it because I've sold thousands of cars doing the same thing.

SUBTLE STATEMENTS THAT ASSUME THE SALE

There's a mile-long list of the subtle statements that salespeople make while assuming the sale. The following represents a small number that salespeople use in a cross section of situations from different fields:

"I'll send the invoice directly to your attention at your office."

"Okay this order form right here."

"Press hard when you okay the order form. There are three copies."

"You should receive the delivery sometime next week."

"You can handle the payments on a quarterly basis."

"I'm putting you down on the monthly pay plan."

"I think you're smart to make a purchase today before the price schedule goes up."

"You're to be congratulated for your wise decision."

"I'll have it gift wrapped for you."

Each of the above comments are made *before* the prospect consents to buy your product. It works so smoothly. You simply assume the customer is going to buy your product. It's not necessary to ask a question such as: "Where do you want the invoice sent?" or "Would you like to make a payment today?" You assume that, and you continue with your sales presentation.

I recommend that you make and memorize a list of twenty subtle statements that assume the sale with your specific product in mind. For example, an insurance agent might say: "I will put you down on an automatic premium loan"; a television salesperson could say: "This set is going to pick up fourteen stations in your home without the use of cable"; a dog food wholesaler could say: "You just wait and see, our products will sell off your shelves like hotcakes." Statements such as these should be in your arsenal for you to draw upon continually.

These statements are sometimes referred to as "trial closes."

Frankly, I don't like this term because it suggests that you're testing to see if the prospect is ready to buy. I believe you shouldn't have to conduct tests—you should simply attempt to close the sale when you think he's ready—each attempt is the real thing, not a test. However, if one attempt to close the sale by assuming the prospect is ready to buy does not work, you merely regroup and continue to offer more reasons why the prospect should make his buying decision on the spot.

For instance, after I ask the prospect to sign an order form and he balks, I don't pay much attention to it the first time. Instead I might explain something, such as why the car is such a good deal at this particular time. I get him to agree with me, and again I ask him to sign the form. If he still doesn't sign, I continue to attempt to close again and again. And each time I feel it is appropriate, I'll make an assumptive statement such as: "I'll have the car ready for you by Wednesday. Would four o'clock be a good time to pick it up?" or "Do you want the undercoating?" As soon as I get an affirmative reply, I hand the order pad to him, and once again I indicate that I want his signature on it. Sometimes, I remain silent and point to the dotted line. Without a word being spoken, he signs it.

Of course, when the prospect expresses an objection, I deal directly with this specific reason why he doesn't want to make a buying decision. After I feel I have satisfactorily answered his objection, again I assume the sale and make another attempt to close.

A LESSON TAUGHT TO EVERY LAW STUDENT

One of the first lessons taught to every law student is: "Never ask a question when you're cross-examining somebody on the witness stand without knowing the answer beforehand." The same lesson applies to selling.

A trial lawyer gets himself or herself into a lot of trouble by asking a question without knowing the answer, and so will you. And never ask a question that requires a yes or no answer unless you're dead certain the answer will be yes. For example, instead of asking, "Do you want a two-door model?" I'd say, "Do you want the two-door or four-door model?" When asking the latter, which is an either/or question, a person can't reply no. On the other hand, if I asked the first, the prospect can easily say, "No."

Here are a few examples of other either/or questions:

> "Do you prefer delivery on March first or March eighth?"
> "Do you want this invoice sent to your attention or to your secretary's?"
> "Do you want to handle this by credit card or by check?"
> "Do you want the red or the blue model?"
> "Do you want it sent by freight or by air?"

As you can see, each of the above questions offers a choice of what action the prospect can take to finalize the sale. Put yourself in the prospect's shoes. It's difficult, after telling a salesperson that you want the blue model, you'll pay by check, and you want it sent to your house on the eighth by freight to then say, "Oh, I didn't say I was going to buy it today. I want to think it over." It's hard because you actually did say you were going to buy by the answers you gave to the above questions.

It's like the trial lawyer who asks, "Have you stopped beating your wife?" This question carries an obvious assumption. (Note the question wasn't, "Do you beat your wife?") To answer the above question as asked, the man on the witness stand must automatically admit his guilt.

A good habit to develop is to say frequently: "Don't you agree..." For instance, "Don't you agree, Mr. Prospect, that this is a beautiful car?" "Don't you agree, Mrs. Prospect, that this is a dream kitchen?" "Don't you agree, Mr. Prospect, that this lot has a view of the ocean that is simply spectacular?" "Don't you agree, Mrs. Prospect, that this mink coat you're trying on will give you a lot of warmth?" "Don't you agree, sir, that this price represents an excellent value?" Again, you ask the prospect to agree with you on questions that will generate a definite yes response.

I think it's especially effective to ask questions that require yes answers when you're selling to two or more people. For example, when a husband, wife, and a half dozen small children were shopping for a car, I'd say to the wife, "Isn't the remote door-lock feature perfect for your family?" She'd always reply yes. Then I'd follow up by saying, "I bet you like the four-door, too," because with their large family, I knew they were considering only four-door models. "Oh, yes, I would only buy a four-door car," she'd say. After a series of comments of this nature, the husband now believes his wife wants to buy because she keeps agreeing with me. By doing this, I've eliminated the reason for him to ask her for her opinion when it's time to close the sale. Next I start working on him to say yes, and soon they both think the other wants to buy and there's no need for them to conduct a family conference when I ask for the order.

This technique works especially well when you're selling to two partners, or for that matter, a group of businesspeople. It is effective to zero in on getting the dominant person to say yes, so the consent of the others will automatically follow. Of course, I recommend that you size everyone up before determining who in the group calls the shots. Generally, this is the only person you have to sell.

GET THE PROSPECT INTO THE ACT

In the automobile business, I get prospects into the act by letting them take the car for a demonstration ride. (I always go with them to answer questions, etc.) By putting customers behind the wheel, they begin to feel as though the car actually belongs to them. And that's exactly the way I want them to feel. I want them to get used to owning my product. Once people feel ownership, closing the sale becomes merely a formality.

A good jewelry salesperson, for example, slips a diamond ring on a woman's finger and observes her reaction. If she likes the ring, the salesperson assumes the sale by saying: "It's just a size too big, but I'll have it made perfect for you. What are your initials, ma'am? I'll have them engraved on the inside of the band for you."

Likewise, a good clothing salesperson who spots a customer admiring a suit on the rack takes it down and says, "Our dressing room is over there. Go ahead and try it on." As soon as the customer comes out, the salesperson leads him to a mirror. "You look terrific in this color."

After giving the customer a few seconds to admire himself in the mirror, the salesperson says, "Let's have the tailor take a look at it." He then nods his head, and bingo, out of nowhere the tailor is putting his tape all over the customer, taking measurements.

"The shoulders are a good fit, but we'll have to take it in just a bit in the back." And he draws some chalk marks on the jacket to indicate where the alterations belong.

"The sleeves are just a little too long," the tailor says, as if talking to himself. "Do you like your shirt cuff to show?" he asks matter-of-factly.

The customer nods with approval.

"Okay, I'm going to take off about this much," and the tailor puts some chalk lines on the cuff.

"The pants need to be taken in, too," he says, and more chalk marks are made.

Notice that the salesperson didn't wait for the customer to say, "I like this suit and I want to buy it." Instead, the salesperson assumed the customer was going to buy when he remained silent and allowed the suit to be marked. *His silence indicated his consent.* After the salesperson and the tailor have gone to so much trouble and the suit is marked with alteration lines, it's not so easy to say, "Oh, I didn't say I was going to buy this suit. I'm just shopping around!"

I remember a time when I was thinking about taking up skiing and took a browse in a ski shop. Before I knew it, they had me trying on boots. Next, I was taken to another department to find the right skis, and then they were sizing me up for binders so my boots would fit properly with my newly purchased skis. "Now, you'll need some clothes to wear, and goggles, and poles, and . . ." It was as if they assumed I was trying out for the Olympics. Those guys were really good!

One of the best examples I know about getting the customer into the act is done at BabyLand General in Cleveland, Georgia, the home of the Cabbage Patch people. Before founder Xavier Roberts began mass-marketing his products, he sold his soft-sculptured dolls at $200 apiece by offering them for adoption. That's right, people had to adopt a baby doll! Working out of a $250-a-month rented frame house that had been remodeled to resemble a small-town maternity ward, every member of Roberts's staff wore a white uniform like those worn by real doctors and nurses. In short, he created an atmosphere that made customers feel as if they weren't buying a doll, but instead were adopting a baby!

If a customer used the word "doll," he or she was quickly corrected: "They don't like to be called dolls."[1] Furthermore, nobody could buy them. They were "up for adoption," complete with birth certificates. Naturally, there were no prices on the dolls. Only adoption fees.

In the adoption room, a group of people could be seen with their right hands raised taking the Oath of Adoption. Members of the staff have maintained that it's not uncommon to see "new parents" with tears in their eyes. It is very common to see proud fathers grin as they accept cigars that say "It's a boy" or "It's a girl."[2]

"Some people come in full of doubts, but within minutes they get right into the swing of things here," explains an LPN. "Sometimes it's the look of a particular baby that appeals to them. Somebody might want a baby with curly red hair and freckles because 'he looks just like my husband.' Then the husband, who's been nonchalant until then, gets interested and starts to look for one with blue eyes and dimples like his wife. Before they know it, they walk out as the proud parents of two!"

"I get a kick out of the way some people hold their newly adopted babies," says a young intern. "The second that baby is in their arms, they act as if it were their own firstborn. You just see the love in their eyes. Even some husbands who were the biggest doubting Thomases have acted that way."[3]

By creating a make-believe *Fantasy Island* atmosphere and playing it to the hilt, BabyLand General was able to get its customers into the act—and when this happened, those Cabbage Patch Kids sold like hotcakes. It's no wonder the Cabbage Patch product was one of the hottest fads this country has ever seen.

While you can see how easy it is to get prospects into the act by letting them participate, to some it appears to be more difficult with an intangible product. Not true! For instance, I've had real estate salespeople tell me: "It's hard to get a prospect into the act when you're selling a parcel of vacant land." I disagree. In fact, when you appeal to an individual's imagination, there's no limit to what you can do to get him into the act.

In selling a residential lot, for example, a good real estate agent says: "Your family room will be right here where we're standing. Just look at this magnificent view you'll have when you're sitting on your sofa. And your swimming pool will go over there on the southern portion of the lot, so you'll get maximum exposure to the sun."

A life insurance agent paints a vivid picture of how his or her clients will live a life of comfort because they had the foresight to plan for the future by purchasing an annuity. The agent sells him the good life by showing how an annuity provides for the future. He has the prospect visualizing himself kissing his wife good-bye and walking out of his Florida condo en route to meeting his buddies at the golf course. Or the agent might choose to project a negative future, a bleak one forecasting the hardships of poverty. By showing the prospect what can happen to him if he doesn't buy, he also gets him into the act. "With the high cost of food," he says, "there are hundreds of thousands of senior citizens in America who are eating dog food to survive. And there's some speculation that social security could go belly-up before you ever reach retirement."

In the above examples, the prospect is brought into the act through his or her imagination. Paint the right mental picture and your prospects will actively participate just as if you had them behind the wheel in a car demonstration.

SOMETIMES DOING NOTHING MEANS YES

I think the real masters of assuming the sale are those companies that *make you do something before you can refuse to buy their products.* For instance, when you rent a car, you're told to put your initials on the application if you don't want the insurance. They want you to think, "I'm not going to sign that. It's just my luck that after I sign, I'll have an accident!" If you've ever belonged to a book-of-the-month, record-of-the-month, or even your favorite-fruit-of-the-month club, they make you notify them only when you *don't* want to buy during a particular month.

Or how about the magazine publishers that require you to write to them to discontinue your subscription? These companies make it hard to stop the sale, and when given a choice, most people take the easy way out. The customers who do nothing are automatically forced to buy the product! Insurance companies assume the sale when they send a renewal premium to you. Did you ever notice that they don't ask you if you want to continue your insurance for another year? Once you're on the books, they assume you're their customer for life, and they keep sending premium invoices to you until the day you die! The insurance companies do it, and their clients never recognize what's happening.

Companies that offer you a ten-day free-trial period employ this same tactic. They send you their product knowing that you're probably too lazy to ship it back to them (of course you must pay the shipping charges). Some make it difficult for you to get their merchandise out of the box without ripping the box to shreds in the process. Consequently, you must find your own replacement box, which generally is an odd shape, again making it hard to return. So, once again, you're encouraged to take the easy route and do nothing—and by default, you're the proud owner of a brand-new _____! Congratulations.

USING THE RIGHT WORDS

There are certain words that assume the sale and certain words that don't. For starters, get used to saying "when" instead of "if." For example, "*When* you own this car, I can promise you that you're going to love it" rather than "If you own this car." See how the one word assumes the sale and the other doesn't? The word *if* raises the question in the prospect's mind: "Well, maybe I'll own it, and maybe I won't."

I also recommend using the first-person plural "we" and "let's." For example, "We should buy fourteen gross at this price," and "Let's place an order for five thousand shares at twenty." By saying it this way, the prospect doesn't feel as if he or she is put in the position of making a major decision on his or her own. You're doing it together, and you lessen the decision-making burden for the buyer. Psychologically, people feel more comfortable making decisions with somebody else because they don't have to take sole responsibility if it turns out to be a wrong decision.

ASSUMING THE SALE ON REPEAT ORDERS

It's always a pleasure to do business with satisfied customers because closing the next sale is much easier. But don't take anything for granted. You have to know how to close these calls, too.

When you're selling customers who already have benefited from your product and service, you assume that because they realize the value of your product, they're going to buy more when it's time to reorder. This is a logical and intelligent assumption.

When calling on a satisfied customer, I recommend that you take the bull by the horns. For example, a dress shirt manufacturer's rep will take an inventory of a men's store and tell the buyer: "You need a dozen more white shirts in size large, a half dozen mediums, and four in the small. Now, in the blues . . ."

Notice that he didn't ask: "Do you want to reorder more shirts to fill in for the ones that you sold?"

Likewise, a stockbroker says: "We have a substantial profit, so now it's time for us to sell two thousand shares of XYZ Company at forty, and with the proceeds we could take a position of eight thousand shares in ABC Company selling at ten." Again, the broker assumed the sale. She didn't ask: "Do you want to sell XYZ Company?" or "Do you want to buy eight thousand shares of ABC Company?"

While I do want you to assume every sale, by no means am I suggesting that you take your existing customers for granted just because they're on the books. You don't own them, and there's always somebody else who can offer them the same thing you do. Once you have a satisfied customer, continue to give outstanding service. In fact, do backbends to keep your happy customers coming back.

4
READING BUYING SIGNALS

I'll tell up front that my views on reading buying signals probably are not what you'd expect. Many people would assume I have a bag full of magic tricks to guarantee sales. But I don't. What's more, I think that anytime you play amateur psychologist, you're treading on thin ice.

I'm not suggesting that there are no buying signals. Of course there are. Who could deny, for instance, that if you're selling food and a prospect drools on your arm, he's sending you a message that he's interested in your product. But in spite of the obvious, buying signals are, at best, subtle and difficult to interpret.

So many myths surround buying signals, which can easily be misread. If you insist on playing psychologist, you'll end up reading more people wrong than right, and ultimately you'll find yourself on the short end of the stick. After all, we are not dealing with an exact science.

Many misguided salespeople believe that reading buying signals is a natural talent that cannot be taught. They claim you're either born with it or you're not. Frankly, it blows me away that some think reading people is in the genes. While some people have the natural talent to paint, compose music, or pitch baseballs, no one is born to read buying signals, any more than people are born to practice dentistry or law or politics. In my opinion, reading buying signals is an acquired skill. It's as simple as that!

BEWARE OF READING
BETWEEN THE LINES

There's a story about a train on its way from Paris to Madrid. One compartment holds four people: a young, beautiful girl traveling with her elderly grandmother, and an old, stately general accompanied by a young, handsome second lieutenant. The foursome is sitting quietly as the train enters a tunnel in the Pyrenees, the mountain range on the border between France and Spain.

It is pitch-dark in the tunnel when suddenly the sound of a loud kiss echoes out, followed by the even louder sound of a hard smack. When the train pulls out of the tunnel, the four people remain sitting silently without acknowledging the incident.

The young girl thinks to herself: "Boy, I sure enjoyed that wonderful kiss the handsome lieutenant gave me. But my grandmother slapped him, so I don't suppose he'll want to try anything again in the next tunnel. Gosh, why did she have to do that?"

The grandmother thinks to herself: "Why, that fresh young man! He kissed my granddaughter. But I raised her properly and she responded by giving him a good, hard slap. I'm proud of her, and I know he'll be sure to keep his hands off her in the next tunnel."

The general thinks to himself: "I can't get over it. My aide went to the finest military schools, and I personally handpicked him. With all his training, he should have known better than to kiss that young girl. But in the dark, the girl obviously thought it was me who kissed her, and I'm the one who got slapped. When we get back to the base, I'm going to give him a piece of my mind."

The young lieutenant thinks to himself: "Gosh, that was wonderful. How often do you get to kiss a beautiful girl and slug your boss at the same time?"

As the above story illustrates, people can arrive at different conclusions based on the same set of facts. For instance, a new salesman once asked me to watch him give a presentation and offer some tips on what he might be doing wrong. He was in a bad slump so I agreed to lend him a hand. I agreed to watch, but the deal was that I wouldn't say a word—I'd be a silent observer throughout the entire presentation. When the salesman reached the point where he began to quote the price of the car, the prospect took out a hand calculator and started writing down numbers on a scratch pad. With this, the salesman became nervous and hesitant. He became so mealymouthed he blew the sale. After the prospect left the showroom, the salesman said to me: "Did you see that?"

"See what?" I asked.

"What he did with his calculator. That guy had no intention of buying a car. He was shopping around, and I bet he'll hit every dealer in town before he makes up his mind. I never have any luck with shoppers."

"No wonder," I said.

I explained that there were probably several dozen different interpretations that could have been concluded from observing a prospect with a calculator. Frankly, my own was that the prospect was obviously interested or he wouldn't have gone through the effort of jotting down numbers. My conclusion was that it was a positive sign, not a negative one. So I caution you to refrain from reading between the lines. There is a great risk of reacting wrongly to what you *think* is a buying signal, or for that matter, a nonbuying signal.

A slew of books have been written about body language and related subjects, and undoubtedly some people do know how to interpret certain signs correctly. These folks know what it means when one person folds her arms a certain way, another crosses his legs, or yet another plays with his beard. But frankly, I'm not that smart. I think that most body movements and facial expressions are unrelated to the sales presentation, and once you start reading between the lines, you'll begin reaching a lot of wrong conclusions. Prospects, like everyone else, scratch their noses because their noses itch and cross their legs to be more comfortable.

I'm familiar with the so-called experts who claim that while people can fool you by what they say, they can't hide the feelings expressed through body language and facial twitches.

They may, indeed, be giving off signals, but I'm not certain that an untrained person can clearly determine what's really going on.

For example, I'm constantly hearing speakers tell their audiences to observe such signs as dryness of the mouth; beads of perspiration on the brow; sweating hands; nervous shuffling of feet; twitching of the eye; a stutter or a mumbling of words; pursing the lips; different tones of speech; raising and lowering the voice; tapping fingers; lifting eyebrows; tugging at an ear; leaning back with both hands supporting the head; index finger placed on temple; removing glasses; biting on a pencil; pacing; jingling money in pockets; biting fingernails; contracted or dilated pupils; or a sudden, nervous cough. You get the point. As I said, I'm not smart enough to tell you that these are definite signals by which you should plan your close of the sale. Furthermore, because some movements can be caused by a variety of circumstances, they could take place during your sales presentation merely by coincidence.

I am not suggesting that you ignore body language altogether. Sometimes it's so obvious that you can't miss it. For example, when a person begins to look around the room instead of paying attention to what you're saying, you're losing his interest. And when the prospect begins to yawn constantly, you are clearly boring him. It doesn't take a degree in psychology to know that unless you get him back on track, you're not going to make the sale.

As I mentioned in Chapter 2, it is important for you to maintain eye contact with the prospect because people interpret this as a sign of honesty. A salesperson who can't look people in the eye is viewed as shifty and dishonest. Note that I didn't say *I* feel this way. But because most people do, I strongly recommend that every salesperson do so. There are reasons, however, why some honest folks don't make eye contact. Some trustworthy people simply are too shy to look anyone in the eye. And in some foreign cultures, it is considered disrespectful to look a superior in the eye. So if a prospect doesn't make good eye contact with you, don't automatically assume that your presentation is going poorly. Once again, don't read between the lines.

AVOID STEREOTYPING

Just as some people misinterpret buying signals, others mistakenly stereotype certain groups of people. There are many false interpretations of ethnic groups—too many for me to get into—and all offensive. My thoughts on this are that you must accept the fact that people are people and don't stereotype ethnic groups. By doing so, you'll only get yourself into trouble. When a prospect has both a need and the money to buy your product, it doesn't matter where his ancestors are from, what color he is, or what his religious beliefs are. And once you start thinking that these things make a difference, it is going to cost you a lot of sales.

The stereotyping doesn't stop here. Some salespeople go so far as to size up prospects according to their occupation. Here are a few examples of what I've heard them tell me about the following:

Accountants	Skeptical and conservative; only interested in the financial aspects of the product.
Dentists	They are thinkers and not impulsive buyers; must be sold strictly with facts.
Engineers	Make decisions methodically and logically; they are interested in numbers; difficult to motivate.
Farmers	Conservative individualists; the salesperson must appeal to their independent spirit; farmers are personable and understanding.
Entrepreneurs	Open-minded and aggressive thinkers; can make quick buying decisions; the salesperson must use enthusiastic presentations and feed their egos.
Executives	Self-motivators, but need guidance because they often lack leadership; the salesperson must play on their egos.
Lawyers	Tend to be experts on all subjects; slow to act; have big egos; like to control.
Physicians	Tend to be prima donnas who like to be

	put on a pedestal; thinkers; don't like to make decisions out of their field of expertise.
Salespeople	Positive thinkers; enthusiastic; will buy when pressured with a strong close.
Technicians	Must be given direction; will react favorably when the salesperson controls the sales presentation.

I obtained the above stereotypes from salesmen, several books I found at the library, and what I've heard speakers tell their audiences. To neatly wrap it up, my first, last, and only rule on the subject is: *Never stereotype.* For those salespeople who do, I'd like to have their professional opinion on how to deal with the black dentist who is Jewish and Italian. And oh, yes, she smokes cigars.

OBSERVE TANGIBLES

While I don't try to interpret the meanings of all facial expressions and body movements, I do pay attention to solid, physical evidence. I believe you can pick up some valuable insight into people's buying habits by observing what they have previously purchased.

For example, when a prospect wearing expensive jewelry and fine clothes would come into my showroom, I would know he or she probably would go for one of the more exciting models instead of a conservative car with no options. Or if I were in the prospect's office or home and observed a lot of gadgets, I would know the person was a good candidate for a car equipped with the works. Everything from the artwork on his walls to the photographs on his desk would tell me something about the man. For instance, original artwork told me the prospect wasn't afraid to spend a sizable sum of money on something he thought represented a good investment. Photos of the wife and children told me he was a family man, which could have a direct bearing on the kind of car he bought. On the other hand, the plain dresser, or the person with no decor in his or her office, probably would go for a stripped-down model. Naturally, these were just hunches, and during the course of the sales presentation I'd remain flexible and close the sale only after I got to know more about the prospect.

Some people like to go first class, while others choose economy. Sometimes it's a matter of how big their pocketbook is, but often it's a matter of lifestyle preference. You must use good judgment or you'll be fooled. Many people have come into my showroom looking as if they didn't have a dime, and then they've paid cash for the most expensive model I had. Again, I warn you not to stereotype.

Depending on what you sell, there may be an excellent advantage to selling on the prospect's turf because it gives you an opportunity to find out a lot more about him. His environ-ment offers many insights into him that you simply cannot otherwise find.

Because I was in the automobile business, it was natural that I'd pay close attention to the prospect's car. I warn you again, however, that some people drive old junkies to knock around in but have more expensive models in their garages at home. What concerns me more than the year and model of somebody's car is the condition it's in. For instance, a car with bald tires, cracked windows, and other unsafe features tells me the prospect probably is suffering hard times. This is particularly true if he's a family man because most people don't expose their loved ones to unnecessary dangers. Of course, you don't have to be in the automobile business to make the same observations about a prospect's car. You can do the same thing regardless of what you sell.

If you sell merchandise to retailers, I recommend that you "shop" their store before you make a sales presentation. For example, a salesperson with a men's clothing line should ob-serve the suits and sportswear displayed in the store. By doing this, you can judge its clientele, price ranges, and preferred styles. For instance, a line of traditional suits may be big sellers for one retailer but bomb in a high-style store. It's important to note that a good retail operation has a theme, and your goods must be compatible with the other merchandise in the store.

Another overlooked but important source of information is an existing account's activities prior to your call. That's right, it's back to doing your homework again. By knowing what a customer has bought in the past, you can better be prepared to sell him or her additional merchandise. By reviewing the books beforehand, you'll probably know more about how your goods are selling than even your customer does.

GET THE PROSPECT INTO THE ACT...AND OBSERVE

As I explained in Chapter 3, the more you get your prospect to participate, the better. When I got the customer behind the wheel, I'd keep quiet and pay close attention to his reactions. Here, I was able to pick up all kinds of buying signals. I could tell from the way one prospect seemed to enjoy driving the car that he wanted to own it. He didn't have to say, "Joe, I want to buy this car," for me to know what was on his mind. Perhaps another customer wasn't reacting the same way, so I'd suggest a different model and let him test-drive that one.

Sometimes I could tell a customer wanted to buy because after the test drive, I'd get out of the car and he'd just sit there and daydream. It was as though he didn't want to leave *his* car. Talk about assuming ownership!

In the same way, a fur coat salesperson can observe clear buying signals when a woman keeps admiring herself in the mirror when she's wearing the merchandise. "I've had some ladies come in here and wear a fur for fifteen minutes on a hot summer day," one salesperson told me. "They parade back and forth in front of the mirror as if they're in a fashion show. They keep rubbing the fur, and tears practically come to their eyes when they have to take it off." These are what I call strong buying signals.

If you pay attention, it's easy to pick up buying signals when the prospect becomes a participant instead of a spectator. When people play with buttons, touch materials, or keep walking back to reexamine the product you demonstrated, they're definitely telling you something. With those Cabbage Patch dolls I told you about, it becomes fairly obvious that it's time to close the sale when a customer picks up her "baby," rocks it in her arms, then says, "Come on, Barbie Sue, give Mommy a nice, big burp."

With intangible products such as insurance, sometimes a powerful, emotional, third-person story will bring tears to a prospect's eyes. When this happens, there's your buying signal; you're getting a clear message to close the sale.

BEING A GOOD LISTENER

When most people think about a sales presentation, they envision the salesperson doing all of the talking and the prospect doing all of the listening. Truly outstanding salespeople, however, also are excellent listeners. In fact, effective salesmanship is based on two-way communication. While you must present your product or service convincingly, the ability to listen is equally important in selling. A professional salesperson must understand how the prospect thinks and feels. As somebody once said, "God gave you two ears and only one mouth, so He meant for you to do twice as much listening as talking."

For some reason, most salespeople equate good selling with the ability to persuade prospects through a constant talkathon. These same individuals consider any pause in the conversation a representation of a flaw in their sales presentation. That's absurd. In fact, a deliberate pause at the right time, or a moment of silence, is a dynamite selling technique.

There's no reason to feel uncomfortable with silence. It isn't true that nonstop talking is a necessary ingredient in a successful sales presentation. I believe that you should allow the prospect an opportunity to think, and let him express his viewpoints. Failure to do so not only deprives you of knowing what he's thinking, but it is often considered rude because you aren't interested in his opinions.

Most importantly, only by listening can you determine what the prospect wants and needs. A real estate agent, for example, can pick up all kinds of buying signals by allowing people to talk. When a prospect mentions that her children are enrolled in private schools, it's a tip to the agent that the quality of the school district is not a major issue. Likewise, when the husband says: "We're not the outdoor types," the agent should consider showing homes situated on small lots.

Stockbrokers must be particularly good listeners because their selling is primarily on the telephone. For example, when a client asks about the dividend history of each recommended company, an observant broker recognizes that he or she should stress income investments instead of growth stocks.

Obviously, certain comments signal definite interest. The following remarks indicate that you are close to closing the sale:

"How soon can it be delivered?"

"It (a computer or other product that generates savings) should pay for itself in a matter of months."

"What are the monthly payments?"

"What colors does it come in?"

"My husband/wife will love it."

"What happens if I push this button?"

"How does this work?"

"If I were going to buy it, how much would I have to pay now?"

"Which do you recommend?"

"What's the difference between this model and the more expensive one?"

"That's a good point. I see what you mean."

"Can I take it home and try it?"

"Do you take trade-ins?"

"Oh, I love this feature."

It's a shame, but many salespeople are so busy gabbing away that they fail to listen to these buying signals. For my money, a top salesperson must be just as skillful at listening as he is at talking. Yet this is one of the most overlooked areas in the field of selling.

It's too bad they don't teach us more about listening in school. I don't know of a single school that has a course in listening. They teach us other forms of communication, such as writing, reading, and speaking, but not listening. Yet every salesperson could benefit by developing this skill.

READING THE "PROFESSIONAL" BUYER

Some people make a profession out of buying. These folks are a special breed all their own, including such people as purchasing agents and merchandise buyers. They make their living by spending eight hours a day buying such things as parts, supplies, or merchandise for their employers, so the buying signals you'll pick up from them are far different from most other buyers.

For starters, these individuals probably know as much about your product as you do. Furthermore, they know how to read salespeople, and *they know you know how to read them*. Knowing this, they'll work hard at covering up what they think could be interpreted as buying signals. After all, they don't want you to know what's going on in their minds because it could become a factor when it comes time to negotiate prices or special terms. These buyers are quite good at hiding emotions, and generally the more nonchalant they act, the more interested they are in doing business with you. But like all other buying signals, some people are simply nonchalant about everything, so here, too, you may pick up the wrong signals.

To illustrate the difference between a professional and a nonprofessional, Martin Seldman, an international consultant who specializes in sales and management training, offers some expert advice on nonverbal communications. Having consulted with gambling casinos, he claims that some definite similarities exist between professional gambling and career buying. "When observing gamblers," Seldman says, "the professionals look for 'tells,' which to the salesperson are his buying signals. Now, the nonprofessional gambler, like the ordinary sales prospect, is not aware that he is relaying signals. But a professional gambler will quickly pick up the tells, such as a flush in the color of one's face, a brightening of one's eyes, or simply a sudden interest in the flow of the game itself. With a poor hand, the nonprofessional gambler becomes bored and restless, but when he's staring at what looks like a winning hand, he becomes turned on. He may begin to ask questions, such as 'What's the maximum amount I can raise?' or 'How many raises are remaining?'

To relate this to selling, it's the same as the customer who asks questions such as 'Do you accept personal checks?' or 'What are the delivery charges?'

"However, the professional gambler knows better than to give his hand away, and sometimes he will act the opposite of what the other gamblers at the table expect. In other words, with a good hand he'll act restless and bored. Now, getting back to selling, I believe professional buyers are as skillful at their jobs as the professional gamblers are at theirs. So remember that when you deal with professionals in any field, you must recognize that they are different from other prospects, and accordingly, you must alter your presentation to them to reflect these differences. If you don't, you'll read people wrong and wind up losing your shirt!"

OBSERVING CUSTOMERS IN SOCIAL ENVIRONMENTS

One of the best times to read people is when they're engaged in social activities. Of course, you may never have an opportunity to get this kind of exposure if your business doesn't warrant it. But if you do meet with your customers on the golf course, tennis court, racquetball court, or at a social affair, you have an opportunity to pick up valuable clues to help you in your selling efforts.

For example, during a mixed-doubles tennis match, a real estate broker told me he noticed that his prospect blamed his wife for every lost point. "It told me that he was very competitive and couldn't stand losing," the broker said. "So when I later sold him a shopping center, I was prepared for him to be a tough negotiator. I also knew that unless he was certain he could get a 'steal,' he wouldn't buy. With this knowledge, I was able to make the sale."

There is also a lot to be learned about people when you observe them at breakfast, lunch, and dinner meetings. For instance, an attorney once told me how he gained some valuable insight about how to deal with a Chief Executive Officer of a large corporation by what happened during lunch prior to the actual negotiations that occurred later that same afternoon.

"The CEO was grossly overweight," the attorney explained, "and stated that he was on a strict diet and would only have a salad with no dressing and a glass of water. In fact, he spent five minutes telling me about how his doctor warned him to stick to his diet. After the waiter came to take my order, I made the simple comment to my guest, 'My mouth is watering for their roast beef. It's the best in town.'

"He looked at the menu once more and said, 'If it's that good, maybe I'll have some, too.' Then he joined me for some strawberry shortcake for dessert.

"I figured if he could change his mind so easily, how firm would he be with his final position during our negotiation? Evidently, he didn't stick strongly to his conviction concerning his diet, so this might be an indication of how he conducted his business affairs, too. As things turned out, we were able to negotiate a lower price three times after he stated his final offer."

STUDY THE EGO

The nice thing about egos is that everyone has one. And the bigger they are, the easier they are to read. But don't get egos confused with being egotistical. A person with a big ego has a high opinion of himself, whereas an egotistical person often acts conceited to cover an inferiority complex. I don't intend to play psychologist, but it does help to recognize a prospect with a big ego.

These individuals believe in themselves and are willing to take risks. I like to do business with this kind of person because they have the self-confidence to make buying decisions. On the other hand, people with weak egos are afraid to take risks, and they hesitate on expensive purchases because they're afraid of making a mistake. With these prospects, it's necessary to control the sale, a subject I'll cover in detail in Chapter 7.

In the automobile business, some believe that the type of car a person drives is an extension of his or her ego. For example, the bigger the ego, the bigger the car. Frankly, this generalization is too broad for me. I've seen too many people with big egos buy small cars, and vice versa. However, certain people do thrive on playing the role of Mr. Big, and these people are rarely seen driving Volkswagen bugs. They're also the kind of prospects that jewelers, clothiers, real estate agents, and gambling casino operators understandably welcome with open arms.

A good friend of mine (I can't mention his real name so I'll refer to him as John) has ghostwritten several books for prominent business leaders and celebrities. In addition to his writing skills, John is an excellent salesperson. "My subjects have huge egos, and some have wanted me to write for a smaller amount than my going fee," he says, "so, during my initial meetings with these people, I must give a good sales pitch to convince them to pay me what I think is a fair percentage of the royalties.

"I do my homework in advance by reading everything I can about them. It's quite flattering to people when they discover that I know so much about their lives, and needless to say, this scores several points for me.

"Perhaps the best way I sell myself is by letting them do most of the talking. You see, people with big egos love having a good audience, so I sit back and do a lot of listening. But I take it a step further. In addition to being a good listener I'll pull out a notebook and pencil and jot down what they tell me—and they love it. I do this, not so much for the information, but for the enormous effect that writing their 'pearls of wisdom' has on their egos. They absolutely eat it up—and I get the percentage I ask."

Taking notes is an excellent way to stroke a person's ego, and you don't have to be a writer to use this technique in practically any sales presentation. It demonstrates your interest about what a prospect says. So again, I remind you to be a good listener—and now, an occasional writer, too. Keep in mind, however, that this technique should only be used during a fact-finding session when you're collecting informal information. It does not imply that you should collect information in a notebook that should be written on an order pad. I bring this to your attention because it is important for you to recognize the difference between the two.

5
HANDLING OBJECTIONS

Selling isn't always smooth sailing, and if you see enough prospects, you're bound to run into your share of objections. But if you took away the objections, salespeople would be reduced to nothing more than glorified order-takers—as I said before, but it bears repeating—and commission rates would be a fraction of their present size, and selling would no longer be a prosperous career. So be grateful for the objections. After all, you don't see anyone getting rich selling tickets in those tiny booths in front of movie theaters.

Don't take this to mean that I enjoy being bombarded with objections. I don't look forward to them any more than you do. But years ago I realized that I had to deal with objections to succeed in sales, and ever since I have confronted them vigorously. I accept them as part of the business. In fact, I'd estimate that 80 percent of my sales during my entire career were closed *after* I encountered at least one objection. As you can see, had I stopped selling every time someone didn't want to buy from me, I would have been knocked out of the business years ago.

One way to reduce the number of objections you encounter is to give a thorough sales presentation. The more complete one is, the more clearly the buyer will understand your offer, which, in turn, will provide him with more reason to make a positive buying decision. There have been times when I tried to give a watered-down presentation because I was trying to make a quick sale in time for my next appointment, or I was simply tired from being overworked. Whatever the reason, whenever I did, I ended up having to answer a slew of objections and as a result, found myself spending more time than if I had given a full presentation in the first place.

Another way to reduce objections is by realizing that some objections are raised with enough regularity to become predictable. After a while, you can prepare yourself in advance by building the answers into your sales presentation so you can address the objections before they're raised. Or you can keep effective answers in reserve to draw upon if seldom-raised objections do happen to pop up.

You must realize that your answer to every objection doesn't have to be 100 percent satisfactory. Isn't it a relief to know that it's not mandatory to have the perfect product for every customer? Just imagine if you had insisted on perfection when you selected your spouse, or if your spouse had sought perfection when choosing you. You both had to settle for a few faults because the other qualities were especially appealing. You can apply this thinking to every aspect of your life. There's no such thing as a perfect career, house, investment—nothing is perfect. Life is full of compromises. If people made choices based only on perfection, nothing would ever be decided.

With this in mind, if your prospect doesn't like every feature of your product, don't assume you've lost the sale. After all, your competition won't have a perfect product, either. When I sold cars, I didn't always have an automobile that was better, feature by feature, than all others. All I needed were enough good features to convince people to buy what I had to sell.

OBJECTIONS ARE EXPRESSIONS OF INTEREST

When I tell salespeople that prospects are expressing interest when they raise objections, I sometimes get looks that suggest I've gone off the deep end. "There's got to be a better way for prospects to express themselves," they tell me.

It would be wonderful if all prospects would sign their names on the dotted lines and whip out their checkbooks at the appropriate time in your sales presentation, but as you and I both know, it's just not that easy. Instead, people can be subtle about letting you know their interest. And sometimes those subtleties go right over your head. Often people will raise objections to gather more reasons to buy. But rather than hanging in there, many salespeople will give up and go on to the next call.

I've always believed that when somebody tells me why he doesn't want to buy my product, he's expressing a willingness to listen to why he should buy. As a matter of fact, I welcome objections in this context because I like people who become seriously involved. It's the individual who listens to a sales presentation and says nothing who's a far more difficult person to sell. He only shakes his head and makes negative comments such as "I'm not interested," "I don't like it," and "I don't want to buy." These are the most difficult sales because he isn't objecting to anything specific. It's as if the sales presentation had no effect on him whatsoever—he doesn't care to challenge the product's value, question your statement on its quality, or ask for proof that it will solve his problem.

People who care about your product, but who aren't convinced enough yet to buy, will vent their objections. I interpret these objections as positive signs that if I properly handle their questions, I will make the sale. For example, a prospect has a computer system, and replacing it with your model will cost him more money. When he says that perhaps he should continue with his present system to save money, he's asking for assurances that he will benefit from buying your model. But if he says only, "I'll stay with my present model," there's little for you to sink your teeth into. Unless you do some probing to uncover his actual objections, the chances of your making a sale are nil.

Examples of objections with hidden requests for additional information are:

Objection: "I don't think this represents the best value per dollar."

Hidden Request: "I challenge you to prove that your product provides an excellent value for my money."

Objection: "This size doesn't appear to be best for me."
Hidden Request: "Prove to me that this *is* my correct size."

Objection: "I've never heard of your company."
Hidden Request: "I want to buy from you, but I need to know that your company is a trustworthy and reliable firm."

Objection: "I'm trying to reduce expenses, so I'm not in the market for anything new."
Hidden Request: "Unless you can convince me that your product is really something that I need, I won't buy."

Objection: "I'm going to shop around and see what else is available."
Hidden Request: "You haven't sold me. Either keep selling so I'll be convinced to buy now, or I'm taking a walk."

Ideally, the prospect will explain why he prefers his present system over yours. For instance, he might say, "My present model has the capacity to process my accounts receivables daily and yours doesn't." Or he might tell you, "XYZ Machines has a wonderful service contract, and whenever there's a problem, they respond within twenty-four hours." With this information, you can zero in on the prospect's objection. Now it's a matter of convincing the prospect of what you can provide: Your computer has more capacity than his present one, and as a result it will save him time, provide more information, better serve his customers, and reduce downtime because your company's average service call is performed within three and a half hours of the request.

When a prospect is getting outstanding service from an existing source, it's naturally more difficult to win the account. Understandably, people are loyal to those uncommonly rare salespeople and companies that take good care of their customers. For instance, a prospect says to a stockbroker: "I'm quite satisfied with my present broker. I've made money with her and she gives me excellent service. Besides, she's a good friend."

Even this statement doesn't mean there's no chance of winning this prospect over. Here, a good response is: "I am happy to know that you're in such good hands. It's nice to hear good things. But I am sure that you will agree that no stockbroker has a monopoly on good ideas, so with your permission I'd like to keep in touch with you. At some time in the future when what I consider an unusual opportunity to take a position in a particular company becomes available, I will give you a call. Certainly you have no objections to my doing this, do you?"

REAL OBJECTIONS VERSUS FALSE OBJECTIONS

For a variety of reasons, people will give false objections rather than telling you why they really don't want to buy. Obviously, unless you know the real objection, you probably won't be able to overcome what's truly bothering your prospect. Bombarding him with facts that have nothing to do with the real objection won't change his mind. For example:

Alan, a stockbroker, is attempting to secure an order for 5,000 shares of ATR Corporation. His client, Sam, who happens to be his neighbor and close friend, voices the objection that he only invests in growth companies.

"ATR had a loss of five cents a share for the year," Sam objects.

"Yes, but the company had a nonrecurring write-off, and our analysts estimate next year's earnings will come in at eighty cents a share."

"I'll believe it when I see it. The company hasn't made any money for nine quarters," Sam says.

In truth, Sam's real objection is that his nephew is now selling securities, and he plans to use him as his broker (he's under strict orders from his wife). However, he doesn't want to hurt Alan's feelings, as he has been his stockbroker for twenty years. Sam simply doesn't know how to gracefully explain to his old friend that he won't be doing business with him in the future. No matter how hard Alan attempts to sell Sam based on the estimated annual earnings of ATR, he will not persuade him to make the investment because those facts have nothing to do with the real objection. Unless Alan realizes that the nephew is the real reason for not buying, and deals with it directly, Sam is not going to give the order to execute a transaction in his name.

There are dozens of reasons prospects express false objections, and unless you are able to weed out the real objections, you will miss out on a lot of sales. For example, a prospect might not know enough about your company but doesn't want to offend you by suggesting that it may be an unreliable or dishonest firm. Instead, he says: "I'd like to sleep on it." In this situation, you might give him several excellent reasons why it is urgent to act now, such as a shortage of inventory, an impending price increase, or a significant loss he will suffer by putting off the purchase. None of these facts, however, will convince him that you represent a legitimate, trustworthy company.

One of the common objections people don't like to express is that they can't afford to buy your product. It's embarrassing to admit they don't have enough money. It hurts their pride. So rather than saying they can't afford it, people have offered me false excuses ranging from "I have a brother-in-law in the business" to "I want to wait until the new models are available." As you can surmise, unless I was able to size up these prospects correctly, I'd talk until I was blue in the face and never overcome their real objections. Once I knew that, I could talk about trade-in allowances, monthly payments, and a variety of other solutions to convince them that they could, after all, afford to buy a car.

Perhaps the best way to recognize false objections is by observing people's reactions after you provide them with solid answers. Generally, their lack of response to intelligent answers is a good clue that they're not telling you their real objection. Take, for instance, the case about Sam's telling his stockbroker,

Alan, that he had no interest in ATR Corporation because he liked growth companies for investments. After several minutes of presenting solid facts supporting his contention that ATR was, indeed, a growth company, Alan should conclude that something else was his client's real objection. After all, he knew Sam was an otherwise reasonable and astute investor and was ignoring the strong selling points that would normally influence his buying decision.

Another clue is that when people throw a series of unrelated objections at you, it's a signal that they're covering up what is really troubling them. Eventually, you must think to yourself: "Nobody can have so many real objections for not buying!" Once you know this, you can begin to ask questions that will reveal the real objection.

If you still can't uncover it, you may want to bluntly ask: "Mr. Prospect, I'd like to ask you to do me a favor." Most people are thrown back by this and will generally reply: "Sure, what is it?"

"I know that this car is perfect for you and it represents an excellent value, but I have a feeling deep inside me that there's something you haven't told me. I'd like to know the real reason you're hesitant to make a buying decision today."

"Oh, I just want to sleep on it overnight, Joe."

"Come on, what is it?"

"It's really nothing."

"Look, you can tell me. What's really the reason you don't feel comfortable buying a car tonight?"

"Well, to tell you the truth, Joe..."—and they come right out with it.

With this information, I can come back with, "I had a feeling it was something like that, and I want you to know how much I appreciate having you be so up-front with me..." Now an otherwise lost sale has become a probable sale.

As you can see, you sometimes have to do some prodding before a prospect will tell you what's *really* on his mind. But you have to find out, and unless you have some fairly good ideas, I don't recommend attempting to guess because you can cover the entire waterfront before you stumble on the real objection. In the meantime, you're liable to voice a few objections that he hadn't thought about—and in the process, open a can of worms.

There are some people who swear up and down that they're not going to be pressured into buying anything—no matter what! And they're determined right from the start that they won't buy under any circumstances. For instance, a man might tell his coworkers, "A life insurance agent is stopping by tonight, but he's wasting his time. No way is he going to sell me." A couple might accept a free vacation from a recreational land developer with the understanding that they will spend three hours of their weekend listening to a sales presentation. They, too, tell their friends, "We're just going to listen so we can enjoy a weekend out of town. We have absolutely no interest in buying one of their units." Likewise, another person tells his friends that he's going to stop in on his way home from work to look at the new models, "but over my dead body do I intend to buy a car."

Often these people fool themselves because they end up wanting to buy but are embarrassed to face the ridicule and flak from those they told they wouldn't buy. It's important to understand this behavior in order to close the sale, and fortunately there are some clues. One is an unusual amount of unrelated objections. Another could be comments such as "I'm really surprised that it's this good" and "So-and-so told me this was a high-pressure outfit, but you're really not, are you?" When you hear remarks such as these, you must give the prospect some extra assurances that he is making a wise decision.

NEVER BACK A PROSPECT INTO A CORNER

An important rule to remember is that you aren't in business to win the battle and lose the war. I've seen salespeople get into arguments with customers, but no matter who wins the disagreement, the sale is lost. Never argue with customers because you'll end up antagonizing them.

Some objections people raise aren't worth discussing. For

example, when a prospect would say to me during the beginning part of my sales presentation, "I'm just shopping around and don't intend to buy a car today," I would ignore the remark. While I thought that he probably was sincere, I knew he'd feel differently after he'd seen what I had to offer. However, most salespeople have a tendency to fire back: "Why do you want to shop around? Everything you could possibly want is right here in my inventory."

Comments of this nature put the prospect on the defensive. He's backed into a corner and feels he must defend his comment. "Well, I *never* buy a car without comparing prices," he insists in self-defense. Then, throughout the rest of the sales presentation, the prospect feels as though he must save face and not change his mind. It now becomes a matter of honor because giving in would be a sign of weakness.

What could have been a passing comment becomes a matter of principle that has been blown out of proportion. When you put your prospects in this position, you are putting yourself in hot water.

A life insurance agent just beginning his career recently told me about a potentially difficult prospect. I knew this young man had the makings of a great salesman by the way he handled the situation. The agent had walked across a wheat field to see a farmer who was operating a tractor. The farmer turned off the engine so he could hear the agent, then became furious upon discovering that his work had been interrupted. The 6'4" farmer said angrily to the 5'6" agent: "I swore that I'd take the next no-good, low-down insurance agent who called on me and throw him right off my property."

Without hesitating, the young agent looked the farmer straight in the eye and said, "Mister, before you try anything like that, you better take out all the insurance you can get."

There was a brief silence, and then a big smile appeared on the farmer's face. "Young man," he said, "let's go over to the house. I want to hear what you've got to sell."

When they entered the house, the farmer put his arm over the agent's shoulder and said to his wife, "Hey, honey, this little guy thinks he can take me," and he let out a big belly laugh. The agent told me it was the easiest sale he ever made.

This incident reminds me of the time I had a man say, "If you try to pressure me into buying a car, I'm going to throw you through that big glass showroom window."

I replied, "It's really a pleasure to make your acquaintance, sir. You know something, I can tell that this is the beginning of a wonderful friendship." And it was. Over the years, I sold him nine cars. Do you see how I handled what was a potentially difficult situation? Rather than starting a fight with the prospect, I won him over with my wit and charm.

OVERCOMING THE SIX MOST COMMON OBJECTIONS

Obviously, there are real objections that cannot be ignored. You must deal with these directly to close the sale. Five basic objections are the most common in every sales field. (Please note that the "I want to think it over" objections have been omitted because they will be covered in the following chapter, "Overcoming Procrastination.")

■ *"I can't afford it."* (This includes all price objections, such as "It costs too much," "Your price is too high," "That's more than I want to spend," and "I can get it elsewhere for less money.")

Don't overlook the possibility that perhaps your prospect really can't afford to buy your product. Some prodding may be necessary to reveal the truth. If he is telling the truth, you can offer a lower-priced alternative.

Many times when prospects plead poverty, they only *think* they can't afford it. Or you might not have provided enough reasons why your product represents an outstanding value. When a person wants a product badly enough, when he knows he will get his money's worth, and when financing is available, the price objection will disappear.

One way to handle price objections is to break the cost down on a weekly, daily, and even hourly basis. For instance, a $15,000 car has a monthly payment of $300, or $10 a day!

When you talk about only $10 a day, the price sounds more affordable.

A copy-machine salesperson, for example, sells a $7,000 model that costs $2,000 more than the competition's. The customer has decided to buy a new copier, so the salesperson talks about the $2,000 difference instead of the $7,000 price. He then breaks the price difference down to $200 a year over the machine's ten-year life. Based on a five-day work week, that breaks down to a price difference of less than 80 cents a day! Next he compares the seconds per copy saved and converts this time savings into dollars saved per year. To do this, he might ask questions such as "What does your average office person make in an hour?" or "What does your lowest-paid entry-level employee make an hour?" After it is determined that these people are paid $4 an hour, the salesperson says: "What it boils down to is less than twelve minutes a day for the lowest-paid employee on your payroll."

Other examples:

"When you break your monthly payments down to $300 a month, Mr. Rodgers, that's less than $10 a day. Are you aware that the car rental agencies get $39.95 a day for this model? Just think of the pleasure you'll get from driving this car. And you deserve it, don't you? If you keep the car for five years, its value will be 65 percent of what you're paying, so what we're really talking about is a cost of only $3.50 a day!"

"This television set costs less than a glass of beer a day, and your entire family will enjoy it an average of eight hours a day every day for years!"

With some business-related products, you must show how the buyer will *profit* by agreeing to buy from you. Observe:

"Yes, Ann, I know this proposal will mean a substantial increase in your advertising budget, but it will generate a huge increase in sales volume, which means higher profits. In short, it will pay for itself many times over again."

"It is true that this computer system represents a major expense, Stanley, but it will reduce your labor costs and free up four of your employees from monotonous and tedious work to move to more productive areas."

"I realize that this security system is expensive, but it will reduce your insurance cost by about eighty dollars a month. When you take this savings into consideration, you really can afford it. Isn't this true, Terry?"

"Yes, this five-hundred-dollar coat is twice as expensive as the blue one, but you love it, don't you? It's the kind of coat you'll wear for the next ten years because its style is so elegantly basic. On the other hand, you'll get tired of the blue one in a relatively short time. When you spread its cost over a ten-year period, it's a terrific value."

"These cast-iron tools cost twenty-five percent more than the others, but look at the lifetime guarantee! The cheaper ones will break in a few years and will have to be replaced. When it comes to this kind of quality, you get far more than you pay for, Roger."

There are also some excellent reasons why it will actually *cost* the prospect money *not* to buy your product, as mentioned below:

A time-sharing salesperson selling recreational condos tells his prospect: "When the cost of your condo over the next fifteen years is spread out by dividing the price of this unit at $12,000, that's only $800 per yearly vacation. After you take inflation into consideration, you'll be spending peanuts for your vacations over the years. I'm not even including the appreciation of your unit. I estimate that this package will double in value during the next five to seven years. With this in mind, your vacations won't cost you anything—it will be as if you're being paid to take them."

Likewise, a private jet, a co-op apartment for business use in Manhattan, and even the purchase of an office building could be sold on the basis that the owner will realize long-term savings rather than spending money by making a buying decision.

■ *"I want to talk it over with my spouse."* (Included in this category are "I want to discuss it with my partner," "I want to run it by my accountant," "I want to review it with my attorney," etc.)

Perhaps the best way to avoid this objection is to make

sure all decision makers are there for the sales presentation. This is done by saying something such as: "Mr. Grant, I will be at your office on Wednesday afternoon at three-fifteen sharp. I strongly recommend that you have whoever is necessary to make a decision present." If he replies, "I'm the decision maker," then it's appropriate to say, "It's a pleasure to meet a person who has the ability to make a decision on his own without a committee to do it for him." This sets the stage so the prospect can't avoid making the decision on his own at the time of the sales presentation.

This technique also works the same way when selling to married couples. "Will it be necessary to have your wife present to share in the decision making, Mr. Masters?" If the answer is yes, you'd better have her there. If he says no, then you say, "It's a pleasure to meet a man who can make a decision on his own." If the spouse is available, you can say: "Is it necessary to have your wife join us at this meeting for a decision to be made? If so, she sure is welcome." Of course, if she's not, let her sit it out.

A lawn-care salesperson told me about an effective way he sells to housewives in the exclusive suburbs of Detroit. "When a housewife says that she has to talk it over with her husband, I ask, 'How much do you spend on groceries each week, ma'am?'

" 'Oh, about two hundred and fifty dollars a week,' she replies.

" 'Do you talk it over with your husband each time before you go to the supermarket?' I ask.

" 'Of course I don't,' she'll say.

" 'Yet you spend more than twelve thousand dollars a year on your groceries. That's quite a big expenditure, and one I notice doesn't require his permission. Well, we're only talking about a two-hundred-dollar-a-month decision, so I'm sure he won't mind your making it, will he?' I then assume the sale by adding, 'Would you like for my crew to come on Wednesday mornings or afternoons?' "

When a potential car buyer told me he wanted to talk it over with his wife at the end of a sales presentation and she wasn't there, I'd say: "In the meantime, let's put the order through. Go ahead and put your okay right here, will you? And I need one hundred dollars as a deposit." The first time he'd say it, I'd ignore the remark rather than making an issue out of it. If the prospect was the macho type, I'd add: "You know something, Harvey, it's a real treat to deal with a man like you who's capable of making up his own mind. There are too many guys these days who let their wives call all of the shots."

If he'd still say, "No, Joe, I have to talk to her," I'd add, "Let's get the order processed and you can go home and tell her about it. Or better yet, bring her down here and let me. If she's against it, you can have your deposit back." In the vast majority of cases, these deals went through. But if the customer walked out without making a deposit, the chances were great that I'd lost the sale because he wouldn't come back. Of course, when a woman comes in without her husband, I naturally tell her how much I admire today's women who make buying decisions without their husbands' permission.

■ *"I have a good friend in the business."* (Or it could be a brother-in-law, a mother-in-law, or a next-door neighbor, etc. who sells the same thing you sell.)

Here you must ask yourself: "Is the prospect interested in giving business to his friend or doing what is best for himself?" Generally, most people want to better themselves rather than making a poor purchase at their own expense.

When a stockbroker hears this objection, he replies: "Harry, I understand how you feel toward your friend. But I am sure you would agree that no one has a monopoly on ideas." The broker lets this thought sink in and continues: "What I am primarily interested in is working with you when interesting opportunities develop—ideas we understand and are watching closely, situations that you and your other sources aren't always aware of. After all, both your friend and I have the same objective—to help you build your capital."

After a prospect admits that a life insurance agent has a better policy than the friend's coverage, the response could be: "I'm sure your friend would want you to do what's best for you, Richard. If he didn't feel this way, then he's not such a good friend after all. Now, let's do what we both know is in your family's best interest..."

■ *"I want to shop around."*

When a prospect tells me this, I ask what other car(s) he has in mind. No matter what make he says—Ford, Chrysler, VW, Audi, you name it—I have a file on it. Let's say he says Audi (it could be any make). Well, for years I've saved all the newspaper and magazine articles on every automaker—all the articles, that is, on anything negative about them. With that, I pull out my Audi file and say, "Here, you read this, and I'll be back in a few minutes." I hand him dozens of articles telling about brakes not working, transmissions falling out, and so on.

The poor guy has to sit in my office and read pages and pages of problems that Audi owners have had. Now am I doing anything that's not ethical? The way I see it, it's no different from a trial attorney pleading a case. When I finally reenter the room, the prospect's face is as white as a sheet, and I say: "What do you think, Fred, do you want to see three more files I have on Audi?" Then I put the order pad in front of him and say, "Here, okay this. I'm probably saving your life!" It's amazing how meekly the prospect signs.

Of course, all salespeople can use this technique, no matter what you sell. Naturally, you have to do your homework and start a file on your competition. One easy way to get some negative information on a competitor is to call your local Better Business Bureau and ask if it has a complaint file on XYZ Company. Be sure to say that you're considering doing business with XYZ Company. If they send you a long file of complaints, you can show it to your customers. If you dig, you're bound to come up with some negative facts about any company. If you can't, then that's the company you ought to see about a job.

In the selling business, it's common for people to shop around until they get what they believe is the best deal. So frequently, after you have spent an hour making a sales presentation and quoted a price on your product or service, the prospect will tell you, "I got you beat."

Many salespeople start a shouting match with a buyer at this point. "You're out of your mind. You can't beat this deal," they scream. This only scares the prospect away. What's more, you may end up challenging the prospect to prove he has you beat. If you let him leave, you might prove your point, but you'll never see him again. It would cost him too much face to come back and admit he was wrong.

Salespeople selling all types of products and services have come up against a bad salesperson, a low-ball con-artist, who quotes prices they know they can't sell at. BEWARE OF UNSCRUPULOUS SALESPEOPLE. They'll cost you time, lost sales, and frustration. These low-ball crooks hope the customer will come back after shopping around, unable to beat their price, and then they cop a plea. Their price, of course, did not include certain items, and the final price is always higher.

Now here's how Joe Girard would handle this kind of character. I would calmly say, "I think somebody has made a mistake. Don't tell me the salesman's name, but what dealership did he work for?" He says, "ABC Dealership." Then I continue, "Here's what I'm going to do for you, sir. I'm going to prove to you that my deal was so fantastic, you're not going to believe it. What's more, I'm going to save you a lot of time by doing your shopping for you."

At this point, I call ABC Dealership and hand the telephone receiver to the prospect so he could hear it ringing. "Good afternoon, ABC," he hears.

I take the receiver from him and say, "Now, this is the place where you got that price, right?" After he acknowledges I called the right dealership, I ask to speak to a salesman.

"Sir, I bought a car three days ago from a dealer in town, and when I went to pick it up this morning, the salesman claims he made a four-hundred-and-fifty-dollar mistake. I am going to tell you what I want, and if you can give me your best deal, if it beats the one I have, I'll come right over and buy a car from you. But if your price is a single penny more than what you tell me on the telephone, I am going to walk out. Is that fair?"

If the salesman tells me to come in or asks for my phone number, I reply, "No, I only want you to give me a price, and if it's better than the one I have, my wife and I will be in this afternoon."

Almost always, the salesman will resist quoting a figure on the phone, but with persistence, he'll give a quote. In these situations, I know I've made such a low quote that nobody is going to beat it. Finally, the salesman quotes $12,700. My quote was $12,200, and I whisper his figure to my prospect, who had been given a low-ball quote of $11,900 from an ABC salesperson.

"Would you please repeat that number to my wife?" I ask, and I hand the phone receiver to the prospect.

"Twelve thousand seven hundred dollars," he says, and I take the receiver away to speak to the salesman.

"Thank you very much," I say, and hang up. Then I turn to my customer and tell him, "See, what did I tell you?" I put my pen in his hand and put it on the order. "Okay this for me," I say matter-of-factly.

Now and then a prospect will pull out a publication showing what appears to beat my deal. "Hey, look at this, Joe. It says right here," he says, pointing to a figure, "that I can buy it for a hundred dollars less than your quote."

He thinks he's going to shock me, but I simply tell him the price he sees can't be bought. It might not include the same options or dealer charges, I tell him, or it might be a bait-and-switch. That's a technique where the published price is very low, but when you ask for that model, the last one's always been sold, and they try to move you up to a more expensive one.

But after I've said all this, I don't ask the prospect to take it on faith. I use the same approach I explained before, calling the dealer and asking for a quote. I don't tell him I've seen his published price, just that I want his best price for this particular model with these particular options, all costs included.

It never fails. I always beat their price. Then I turn to the prospect.

"Put your okay right here," I'd tell him.

■ *"Leave me some literature, and I'll get back to you."*
Obviously this prospect is letting you know that you haven't convinced him to buy. But don't expect literature to do a better job of closing the sale than you, the salesperson, can do. If that were the case, companies would terminate their sales forces and replace them with mail order departments!

My standard reply to this remark is: "Sure, I'll be happy to give you some brochures about your car. You can show them to your friends who ask about the beautiful new car you're driving." This statement assumes the sale and doesn't accept the idea that the prospect wants to put off making a buying decision. Then, I follow up by giving him more reasons why he should buy the car today. With one buyer, I might reemphasize a few of the features that he particularly liked; with another, I might stress the good trade-in price we will give him for his present car; and with yet somebody else, I will stress special financing terms that I could get for him today. Keep in mind that I might mention all of the above during the same presentation—and several attempts to close will be included.

Perhaps another prospect doesn't let me get away with my show-the-brochures-to-your-friends line. He presses me: "Look, Joe, I haven't made up my mind. That's why I want some literature to take home. So I can decide what I want to do."

With this prospect, I am more direct. I say: "If brochures could do what I'm paid to do, I'd be out of a job. Now, if there is anything that is not clear, that's what I'm here for. Exactly what don't you understand?" If he doesn't express a definite objection, again I continue to give him more reasons for buying.

■ *"I don't want to buy your product because . . ."*
I welcome objections that specifically state what the prospect doesn't like about my product. It allows me to focus on what it would take to get him to buy.

For instance, a prospect might tell me he likes a particular model in a four-door after I've told him that the dealership had only the two-doors in inventory. With this information, I can narrow his objection to one last reason for not buying.

"Gosh, Eddie, we're clean out of the four-door models," I say with a worried look on my face. "And you'd buy the four-door right here on the spot, I bet, if it were available. Isn't that right?"

"Yeah," he'd say with a smirk on his face.

"I don't know what's wrong with me today, Eddie!" I say, slapping myself in the head. "You see, we have an arrangement with four other dealerships in town whereby we use each other's inventory when we're in a bind. We set up this dealer's association so we could provide the best possible service to the customer. We get cars for them and they get cars for us. It all evens itself out, and the customer is the big winner. Give me five minutes, and I'll get you just what you want. You want it in white, but you'd settle for your second choice in black, right?" Then, without waiting for him to reply, I'd turn my back to him and walk over to the telephone and dial the other dealer.

Practically every specific objection can be handled this way as long as you do have a solution to the prospect's problem. Note how isolating the objection to one final problem works with the following products:

"Now, am I to understand that you'd apply for this life insurance policy if it has a provision that would pay your premiums if you were disabled?" a life insurance agent asks. Once the prospect agrees to his one last objection, the agent explains how the waiver of premium will solve the problem.

"Now, am I to understand that your reason for liking XYZ Company's word processor is the fast printer, and you would buy ours if it printed faster?" Upon getting the prospect to agree, the salesperson explains how it is possible to get a compatible, faster printer from another company.

"Now, I don't know if I can do it for you, but if our trade-in department would give you seven thousand dollars on your car, you say that it's definite that you will buy this new one today?" I used this technique knowing in advance that the trade-in would be $7,000. But I'd act as if it were going to be extremely difficult to cut such a deal. "Well, I seriously doubt if they'll give you such a large allowance, and if you do get it, you got the deal of a lifetime. But I don't suppose there's any harm in asking. Let me see what I can get for you . . ."

A real estate agent says: "The asking price is $300,000, but am I to understand that you'd buy this house for $250,000? I don't blame you, but I'd be amazed if they'd sell it at this price." In the meantime, the realtor knows in advance that the seller has said he would take $250,000. "Well, I'm going to write up an offer for $250,000 and we'll just have to keep our fingers crossed." He writes the figure on the contract and says, "Now okay this for me right here, and I'll submit it for you."

"Now, am I to understand that your only reason for not buying today is that the suit feels too big in the midsection? Gosh, Jim, you know we don't have it in the next size." Once the prospect agrees he would buy if the suit fit better, the salesperson calls for the tailor to do some alterations so the suit will be a perfect fit. (The salesperson already knew the tailor could make the alterations.)

"I DON'T HAVE THE MONEY AT THIS TIME"

Every now and then a prospect would be shopping around for a car, and even though I had him sold, he would claim he didn't have a blank check, cash, or a credit card on him to make a down payment. After having spent an hour or so making a sales presentation, I wasn't about to let him walk out because I knew the odds were slim that he'd come back. Besides, I know people only say they don't have any money on them—but in truth, they're not likely to leave home with empty pockets.

Figuring that a bird in the hand was easily worth two in the bush, I'd say: "No problem, Fred. I can't tell you how many times I've done the same thing and walked out of the house without a dime on me." I'd pause for a moment, and I could see that the prospect felt as though he was off the hook and was obviously relieved. Then I'd continue, "In fact, you don't need any money because your word means more to me than all the money in the world."

Then I'd grab the prospect's hand and say, "Just okay this right here," as I placed it over an order form.

Afterward, I'd repeat how good I was at having the right first impression of people, and I knew he'd never let me down. In truth, rarely did people disappoint me when I'd say this to them. I've always found that when you trust good people, they want to prove that your confidence in them was sound. You don't have to sell cars to use this approach. It's just as effective when somebody says, "I'm sorry, but I'm cash poor now. If you see me at the end of the week, I'll have the money."

ANSWER THE OBJECTION AND CLOSE THE SALE

Once you believe that an objection has satisfactorily been answered, briskly move on. It's not necessary to dwell on it by asking such questions as "Well, what do you think now?" or "Does that settle your problem?" You don't need confirmation. Assume it.

It's not your job to show anyone how smart you are, especially at the risk of making your prospect feel inferior. To do so generates ill feelings. So don't start puffing your chest as if to say, "Well, wasn't I simply marvelous in how I answered your objection?" Remember that your mission isn't to win battles and lose the war.

Instead, let the prospect feel as though you served him by providing needed information so he could make an intelligent decision. You should also praise him for his comments and observations. After all, you don't want him to feel as though he has been talked into buying something against his will. So make him feel good about giving his consent after he had initially voiced an objection. Then when all barriers have been removed, you can move on to close the sale.

6

OVERCOMING PROCRASTINATION

In my discussion in the previous chapter I purposely omitted the number one objection that rattles more salespeople than all of the other objections combined. Anyone who has ever sold anything knows exactly what I am referring to—the *"I want to think it over"* objection!

It might not be said in those exact words, but the message is the same when the words are:

> "I want to sleep on it."
> "I never make up my mind on the first call."
> "I want to mull it over."
> "Why don't you call back tomorrow (the first of the month, after the holidays, etc.) and I'll let you know."
> "Give me your card, and I'll call you when I make up my mind."

You get the picture. The prospect simply doesn't want to make a buying decision, and it's not necessarily because he objects to you, your company, or your product. Had he resisted you on any one of these accounts, it would be relatively easy to overcome his resistance. But it's a different story when he takes a dead-center position, straddling the fence without giving you a decision.

WHY PEOPLE PROCRASTINATE

Assuming that you have presented all of the facts that are necessary for the customer to make a buying decision, one reason for procrastination may remain. The customer is afraid of making the wrong decision. He or she would rather take the easy way out and do nothing.

Did you ever notice how fast highly trained and skillful people will react when they're in their own area of expertise? For example, top surgeons make split-second decisions at the operating table because the smallest hesitation can cause a scalpel to slip and bring certain death. Leading NFL quarterbacks must react just as fast during a broken play when 280-pound linemen are furiously rushing at them. And traders on the stock exchange floor make instant decisions with millions of dollars at stake. Yet once removed from their familiar surroundings where they have been trained to perform with precise timing, these same men and women are unable to make what, in comparison, appear to be minor decisions.

Do you see what I'm getting at? So for good reason I've concluded that procrastination is mainly the result of insecurity. People simply don't want to make a decision today and take the risk that it might not be the right one. On the other hand, I've never known anyone to procrastinate when he or she *knew* that buying was absolutely the right thing to do. If you learn nothing else about closing sales, I want you to remember for the rest of your life that *people put off until tomorrow only those decisions they lack the confidence to make today.*

INDECISIVENESS AND DECISIVENESS ARE CONTAGIOUS

It's been said that nothing is as contagious as enthusiasm. I disagree because hesitation, which is the opposite of enthusiasm, is equally contagious.

The old monkey-see, monkey-do adage is so appropriate in closing sales. Just as prospects mimic your enthusiasm, so do they mimic your hesitation. I've seen more salespeople than I care to remember who blew sales because they lacked the self-confidence when it was time to execute their closes. What happens is that they begin to hem and haw. I suppose it's because they can't take the rejection, so they become gun-shy. Once fear sets in, it shows all over—in their eyes, in their facial expressions, and in their body language. Sometimes it's not so obvious and prospects aren't entirely aware of what's going on. But subconsciously, they pick up these vibes, and they, too, begin to hesitate. They hem and haw and become consumed with doubt. Then it's not long before those dreadful words are blurted out: "I want to think it over, and I'll get back to you."

I'm sure you've been on the buyer's side and have observed a salesperson overcome with the jitters when asking for the order. "P-put your J-John Hancock right there," he says hesitantly, his hand shaking as he hands you his pen.

Even though he said the right words, it was the way he said them that gave you doubts about making your buying decision. Up until this moment, you were on course to buy his product. But then you began to feel just a bit unsure. Then you heard yourself mumbling, "I think I'd like to sleep on it." Those words surfaced before you even had time to think of them, and from that point on, your mind-set was geared to giving the matter some thought and getting back to the salesperson in a day or two. What happened is that just as the salesperson was indecisive in asking for the order, so were you indecisive in your response.

On the other hand, some salespeople radiate self-confidence. They ooze it. So what happens? They generate decisiveness. When they call on prospects, they *know* they're going to close sales, and their prospects know it, too. For this reason, you often see one salesperson sell rings around another salesperson even though both give the same word-for-word, canned presentation.

Just as one salesperson makes you feel unsure of yourself, another inspires you with confidence. Here again, he is full of self-confidence and it rubs off on you. For instance, I remember a time early in my career when I went into a travel agency just to inquire about how much a long weekend vacation to Las Vegas would cost. I happened to pick up a brochure on Hawaii, and a saleswoman approached me.

"Have you ever been to Hawaii?" she asked me.

"Only in my dreams," I said.

"Oh, you'll love Hawaii," she said. As the saleswoman showed me some literature, I was impressed with her eagerness to serve me. She painted a vivid picture about how much my wife and I would enjoy the gorgeous beaches. "You're going to have the best time of your life," she said convincingly.

When the saleswoman noticed how I winced as she quoted the cost of a ten-day vacation, she calmly asked, "When was the last time you had a vacation, Mr. Girard?"

"I can't honestly remember when," I commented, not wanting to admit it had been many years.

"You owe it to both you and your wife," she said with a smile. "Life is too short to work as hard as you do and not reward yourself. Besides, you'll feel so good when you return, you'll make it up in no time by selling more cars. I *know* you'll be way ahead in the long run. The much needed rest will do wonders for you."

She spoke with such confidence that I had no trouble making up my mind right on the spot to take the vacation. Yet, I walked in without any thought about a trip to Hawaii.

YOUR JOB DESCRIPTION INCLUDES HELPING CUSTOMERS

Some salespeople lose sight of the fact that part of their mission is to help customers. Yes, you heard me right. Your job description includes helping customers. First, you must inform prospects about how they can benefit from your product and how it represents a good value for their money. Second, you must help them make the proper buying decision. And third, you must service them. (I'll discuss this third part of your job description in detail in a later chapter.)

What it all boils down to is that you do a grave disservice to your prospects when you let them hang on the fence, unable to reach a conclusion. Think about the times you entered a dealer's showroom, for example, to buy a car. About an hour later, you walked out in a state of confusion. Perhaps you weren't even aware of what was bothering you, although you did know that you were feeling disappointed and unfulfilled. You wasted your valuable time and felt as if you were no better off than you were when you first walked into the showroom. Personally, I think any time somebody walks into a retail store and walks out empty-handed, he or she is bound to feel somewhat disappointed. The same holds true when a salesperson calls on a prospect who sets aside his valuable time in anticipation of having a problem solved. If the sale isn't closed, the problem hasn't been solved. Say, for example, a pharmacist is interested in purchasing a system to computerize his accounts receivable and customers' prescriptions. He is aware of how other pharmacists have benefited from the time-saving feature offered by a computer system. Furthermore, the pharmacist realizes that he can no longer delay the decision to make the conversion; his obsolete manual system simply isn't doing an adequate job. He is ready to buy and anxiously sets aside a period during which time a computer company representative will deliver a two-hour presentation. However, the rep makes such a poor attempt to close the sale that the pharmacist becomes confused. His confusion causes indecisiveness, and the sale is not closed. Under this scenario, imagine his frustration and disappointment.

And still another reason why you are doing your customers an injustice by allowing them to procrastinate is that delayed decision-making is often costly. In the case of the above-mentioned pharmacist, the tedious, time-consuming manual system is not only inefficient, but requires considerably more manhours.

While I'm on the subject of helping customers, some procrastinators lack the self-confidence to make a decision without talking it over with a third party, such as a business associate or spouse. This type will say: "I have to discuss it with my wife (partner). I'll review your proposal with her and get back to you tomorrow. I really want to buy it, but you know how it is. She'd give me all kinds of hell if I didn't talk it over with her."

Naturally it would have been better to have the wife there in the first place. But this is something you don't always know, nor can you, with every prospect until after the fact. However, if, in fact, you do determine that he is incapable of making a buying decision on his own, I advise you to say: "I understand exactly what you're talking about. But there's one thing I must insist on doing for you . . ."

"What?" he asks.

"I want to stop by your house this evening, and I want you to let *me* explain it to her. This is my profession, and if she has any questions to ask you when I'm not present, you may not be able to answer them. And it wouldn't be fair to either of you to have her decide without knowing all of the facts." In cases like this, you never want to have a well-meaning prospect try to do your selling for you. Imagine how unconvincing an unskilled salesperson would be at your job, and that's how ineffectively a prospect would sell your product to a third party. And another thing, when you do give your presentation to the third party, give a complete presentation from start to finish; don't give a scaled-down version.

SETTING THE STAGE TO AVOID PROCRASTINATION

I touched upon this technique in Chapter 5 when I told you to request that all decision makers be present at the sales presentation. In a similar way that you set the stage to have a spouse or partner present, you should do the same when you begin your presentation. Be up-front with prospects, and say that you expect them to be able to make a decision after you have presented all the facts.

For instance, after I'd exchanged small talk with a prospect before my sales presentation, I'd say to an executive or entrepreneur: "I really enjoy talking to a person like you. It's a pleasure to see somebody come in here with the ability to make a decision. You wouldn't believe all these guys who come in here who are too meek to make a decision to buy a car."

Do you see what I did? I'm setting the prospect up to know that I expect him to make a decision. Once a prospect is agreeing with me that most people are too timid about making up their minds, I put him in the mind-set to behave as a decision maker. What's more, it would be awfully embarrassing for anyone to tell me at the close of my sales presentation that he was one of those wimps who couldn't make up his mind.

Another way to set the stage for avoiding procrastination at the close of the sale is to stress how valuable time is—the prospect's and yours. For example, an insurance agent calling on a businessperson might say at the beginning of his presentation: "It is a pleasure to meet with a woman such as you, Rita. I know that as the owner of several fast-food franchises, you're a very busy person—and because I appreciate how valuable your time is, I'm going to get right down to business. I'm sure you realize that my time also is valuable. So, with this in mind, I'll explain all of the facts of this program to you in explicit detail, and if you have any questions, I will be delighted to answer them. At that time, if you feel as though this insurance program meets your needs and your budget, I expect you to tell me. On the other hand, if you feel as though it doesn't, please tell me that, too, and I'll be on my way. However, I do expect you to give me a decision today. Fair enough, Rita?"

In another incident, a salesperson might say to an executive: "Now, before I begin, you *are* the person I should be talking to, right?" He then adds, "Now, am I to understand that you have the authority to make a yes-or-no decision today?" Of course if the prospect says no, then the salesperson knows there's no point in giving the presentation.

Even a door-to-door vacuum sweeper salesperson can effectively use this technique by saying: "Let's make an agreement, Susan, one that I think you'll like. I'm not one of those high-pressure salespeople, so you don't have to worry about me trying to sell you anything you don't want. All I want to do today is demonstrate my vacuum sweeper and show you how a lot of your neighbors and friends have benefited from it. Then, if you think it's something that will make your life a lot easier, and if you feel it's something you can afford, I want you to buy it and be one of our customers. And if you don't feel this way, I don't want you to buy it. Now is that fair enough?"

Rarely will anyone disagree to be decisive when asked before the presentation to make a decision to buy. And by doing this in the beginning of the interview, procrastination is held to a minimum when it's time to close the sale.

APPEALING TO YOUR PROSPECT'S EGO

In Chapter 4, I told you to study egos, and in overcoming procrastination, knowing your prospect's self-opinion is quite useful in closing the sale. In the same way you prepared the prospect before the presentation to make a yes-or-no decision, you must elevate him to feel so important that he's embarrassed to appear wishy-washy when decision time comes. You do this by feeding on a prospect's self-importance and by playing on his vanity.

Men are especially vulnerable to saleswomen who use this technique. For example, a woman selling dictating equipment to a man says to him: "I call on the leading business leaders in town, so I know how a top executive like you values his time, Mr. Mitchell. I am sure you will agree with me on this point."

"That's right, young lady. Time is money," Mitchell pompously replies.

"I appreciate how valuable your time is, sir, and because it is, I want to conserve as much of it as I can. For this reason, I want to submit this order today so your machine can be delivered this Friday."

"That's fine, but I'm leaving on a four-thirty plane this afternoon, and I'll be on the road for the next three days, so I really don't want to do anything today. I've got an important meeting on the coast involving a major contract for my company. Now, if you'll leave me a brochure, I'll read it on the plane, Carol..."

"Oh, I know how many things you must have on your mind, Mr. Mitchell, and I'm sure such a relatively minor item like a dictating machine isn't something you'll have time to think about. You shouldn't even have to clutter your mind with this sort of thing. So let's get this order processed while you're on the road and I'll make sure that when you return, your dictating machine will have been delivered so you can begin to use it next weekend."

"That would be nice."

"Please put your name on this line, Mr. Mitchell, and right here on this line, too," she says, assuming the sale.

Another woman selling real estate to an executive who's in the process of being transferred out of town says: "How many times have you been transferred to a new town during your career, Mr. Green?"

"Believe it or not, this is our eleventh move in the past eighteen years."

"Then you're an old pro at it, aren't you?"

"It's a piece of cake," Mr. Green says smiling.

"Good, because it's easier working with a man such as yourself who knows how to buy a home than an executive who has never made an out-of-town move and is scared to death to make a decision without his wife."

I have often used a similar line to build up a woman's ego. I'd say: "I admire today's strong women who are capable of making decisions that were unthinkable for women to make just a generation ago."

"That's right, Mr. Girard," young women barely past their teens have told me, "and want to know something else? In her entire lifetime, my mother never even went into an auto dealer's showroom by herself!"

This same approach works well when a young salesperson calls on a prospect who is several years older. The salesperson uses his youth as an advantage by saying, "I enjoy talking to experienced individuals like you who are capable of making decisions. You know, too many young people today don't know how to make up their minds."

You can use this line on practically anyone to build up high self-esteem. Big egos aren't limited by age or gender, nor are they only possessed by people in high positions.

"I WANT TO THINK IT OVER"

In the rest of this chapter I'll discuss what to say to the prospect who declares at the tail end of your sales presentation: "*I want to think it over*." Because procrastination is a trait common to most people, you're sure to have your share of these prospects. And unless you have the skill to close a fair percentage of them, your chances of succeeding in sales are limited.

One of my favorite replies to a husband and wife who told me they wanted to think it over was to say: "Do you know what? You people are just like my wife and me."

"We are?" they'd reply. "How's that, Joe?"

"We like to talk things over before we make a decision, too. And I want you to think it over because I don't ever like to have my customers feel they're being high-pressured. As a matter of fact, I'd rather not do business with you than to have you feel that I used high-pressure tactics. Now, don't get me wrong, I do want your business, but it's important to me that you walk out of here with a good feeling."

"We're glad you feel that way, Joe, 'cause to tell you the truth, we'd never buy anything from a car salesman who used high-pressure tactics."

"That's good. I'm glad to hear that. I want the two of you to take your time and think it over." Then I'd shut up and sit back in my chair.

"Say, Joe, wh . . . do you mind?" one of them would say. "This isn't what we had in mind."

"Gosh, I'm sorry. Yeah, sure, I know what you mean. You want to talk it over in private, don't you?"

"Yeah, Joe . . ."

"Sure, you go right ahead," I'd reply. "In the meantime, I'll be in the office next door making a phone call. If you need me, give me a holler. Take your time. There's no hurry."

Of course, I knew "thinking it over" to them meant a lot longer than just a few minutes. What they had in mind was a matter of days, not minutes. I'd give them ten minutes to be alone, then I'd come back and assume the sale by saying something like, "I have some good news for you. I just found out that the service department could have your car prepped by late this afternoon..." See how I assumed the sale?

Often an appropriate quote will motivate a prospect to make a decision. The old cliché "Don't put off to tomorrow what you can do today" is perhaps the most obvious and overused of them all, but even it, at the right moment, makes a statement. A timely quote is effective because it is as if a wise third party steps in to serve as an arbitrator and voices his or her opinion (which naturally favors your point of view). I've seen many sales that could have gone either way go in favor of the salesperson who had the resources to say the right words of wisdom at the appropriate time.

If you do use quotes, I suggest that you pick and choose those that you feel comfortable with. Here are some that deliver a good message and that seem tailor-made for the procrastinator:

"Nothing will ever be attempted if all possible objections must first be overcome."
—SAMUEL JOHNSON
(English literary leader, 1709–1784)

"Do not wait; the time will never be 'just right.' Start where you stand, and work with whatever tools you may have at your command, and better tools will be found as you go along."
—NAPOLEON HILL
(Author of *Think and Grow Rich*)

"Where there is no vision, the people perish..."
—*The Bible*, Proverbs 29:18

"The next day is never so good as the day before."
—PUBLILIUS SYRUS
(Roman statesman, 43 B.C.)

"No decision is difficult to make if you get all the facts."
> —GEORGE S. PATTON, JR.
> (American general during World War II)

"Ask yourself constantly, 'What is the right thing to do?' "
> —CONFUCIUS (Chinese philosopher
> and moral teacher, 551?–479 B.C.)

"A journey of a thousand miles begins with one step."
> —LAO-TZU (Chinese philosopher
> and founder of Taoism, born 604? B.C.)

"He who has begun is half done."
> —HORACE
> (Roman poet, 65–8 B.C.)

I recommend that you have a list of these and other quotes typeset, and keep it with you at all times in your wallet or briefcase. Sometimes the printed word is more "official" than the spoken word, so it's not necessary to memorize these quotes. You can pull these quotations out and hand them to your prospect to read.

It's important to realize that when somebody procrastinates in making a buying decision, it's because you haven't convinced him that it's to his advantage to act now. With this in mind, here's a close that's regularly used by a successful insurance agent that clearly demonstrates the advantage of acting now versus later:

The prospect had told the agent, "I want to think it over."

The agent replied, "If I gave you a feather to put in your pocket, Bruce, and you had to carry it everywhere you went, do you think you'd even feel that the feather was there?"

"I'm sure I wouldn't."

"What if I gave you a round ball of feathers to put in your pocket, and you always had to carry it around wherever you went. You'd probably have an awareness of the bulge it created, wouldn't you?"

"I'm sure I would."

"Now, let's carry it a step further, Bruce. Let's suppose I gave you a king-sized feather pillow, and you had to carry it wherever you went. Don't you think it would be quite a burden to lug around all the time?"

"Yes. But what are you telling me?"

"This small premium at your age today won't make a dent in your pocketbook or in your standard of living. If you elect to wait a few years, you'll have a bigger burden, and a few more years later, you'll have a tremendous burden. Don't you see, Bruce, the time to start this program is today while the burden is so small that it won't make a dent."

As a final technique to overcome the "I want to think it over" objection, here's a direct-to-the-point, no-nonsense close that I've used with much success, one that can work selling practically any product:

"Look, Jack, you and I have spent a couple of hours together, and we both know that this is the right car for you. What's more, you're getting a great deal. There is no reason why you shouldn't buy today, so the only way I'm going to allow you to walk out of here is as my customer. Go ahead now and sign the contract, will you?"

7

CONTROLLING THE SALE

The image that instantly comes to mind when most people think about controlling the sale is one that portrays manipulation and intimidation. I shudder when I think there are salespeople out there using selling techniques that dictate mistreating customers. What's more, I can't imagine anyone's actually getting away with it. Customers should be cherished.

However, I believe a salesperson must be able to control sales presentations, and if not, it is highly probable that problems will surface when it's time to close. In fact, if a salesperson doesn't take charge, I don't think he or she can have a successful sales career.

A TEACHER/PUPIL RELATIONSHIP

Like the caring teacher, I do everything I can to make it crystal clear that I have my customers' best interests in mind. I educate them on the benefits of my product, and then I guide them in the buying-decision process. Sure, sometimes I have to exert more guidance with some prospects than others. With some, my sales presentation runs with clockwork precision as if both the buyer and I were following a script. Then, with others, people require more motivating to make a buying decision. They want to buy but get the jitters about parting with their money. If I were to allow these sales presentations to get out of control and lack direction, I would be negligent in my job. If customers floundered and remained indecisive, I would feel as though I had performed a disservice to them.

While I refer to it as a good teacher/pupil relationship, you may also view it in the same vein as the relationship that a good parent or clergyperson establishes. It's a role of authority, which, when properly sustained, fosters respect and admiration. This is a status that few salespeople ever attain, and one, I believe, that represents a standard that all should seek.

When a top life insurance agent masterfully executes this form of control, he does it to serve his client. What's more, the client appreciates it. Like a professor teaching his student, the agent says: "Many changes have occurred in the industry during the past few years, so if you don't mind, I'd like to take a few minutes to review some of them that I consider to be pertinent to your situation . . ." With this preface, he might then explain what benefits can be derived from universal life insurance, why the prospect might be interested in buying term insurance and investing the difference, and so on. "Now let me tell you about some important tax revisions that I think you should know about," he continues.

Later in the presentation, he adds, "I want to ask you some questions to learn some things about you, and then I'll make some recommendations." Here, his questions might be: "What is the exact nature of your work?" "What is your estimated annual earnings?" "What provisions have you made for your children's education?" "What provisions have you made for your estate taxes if you were to die prematurely?" "For what reasons have you seen a doctor in the past five years?" Notice that even when it comes time for the agent to ask the questions, it is reminiscent of the teacher giving an oral examination to his or her student. When control of this nature is properly executed, it represents a high level of professional selling.

SELLING WITH INTENSITY

Once I'm eyeball-to-eyeball with a customer, you can be sure of one thing—he's going to get my undivided attention. I block everything else out of my mind—I won't allow any thought to distract me. From the moment I shake his hand and introduce myself, nothing can take my attention off my prospect. Five fire engines could race past the showroom, and my head wouldn't turn. I mention this because I've observed other salesmen rush to the window at the sounds of a siren or an auto-mobile crash. And I've seen others with their eyeballs bulging out of their sockets as they admire the pretty pair of legs on a customer at the side of the showroom! If I lived on the West Coast, a massive earthquake wouldn't unglue me from my prospect.

Why is this so controlling? For starters, because I focus in on the prospect with such intensity, I'm watching and listening to every move and sound he makes. But I have to confess, I didn't always treat my customers like this. It's not that I didn't attempt to, but rather a case of lacking an awareness, and consequently allowing outside distractions to take my attention away.

Fortunately, it only took one lost sale to teach me a valuable lesson that has, over the years, resulted in many additional sales. Early in my career, a successful, self-made contractor, who had little formal education, was in my office and was interested in buying a top-of-the-line model equipped with everything. In the middle of the sale, the man began to tell me about his son, Jimmy, a premed student who was attending the University of Michigan. He was obviously proud of his son, but while he was talking to me, I became distracted by a group of salesmen who were standing outside my office, engaged in an unusually loud bull session. I didn't shut the door, and as I listened to the man tell me about his son, I couldn't help overhearing the joke-telling and laughter. Although this was annoying, I kept nodding my head as the prospect boasted about how his son had made the dean's list, participated in sports, and so on. I thought he would feel as though I was really into what he had to say.

However, once we started talking about what was the right car for him to buy, I sensed that the prospect was cooling off, and how soon I found out that I was so right. He abruptly stood up and said, "Mr. Girard, we've talked long enough," and with those words, he walked out. That was the end of the conversation. Period!

In the evenings, when I get home, I often meditate on what I did right and wrong for the day. That night I couldn't get my mind off this particular presentation. So I decided to give the prospect a call at his home to find out what went wrong.

"What happened today," I asked him, "that caused you to walk out like you did?"

"Nothing," he replied, "except that I bought a car from somebody else."

"You what? Why did you do that?" I asked. "I had a terrific deal for you." Then I asked meekly, "Did I do something wrong?"

"What makes you ask me this question?" he replied.

"Well, I'm always interested in bettering myself, and if I said something that offended you, I'd like to know so I won't make the same mistake again."

"I'll tell you what you did wrong, Mr. Girard," he said in a stern voice. "You kept looking out the door and were obviously more interested in hearing those salesmen tell jokes than you were in listening to what I had to say about my son. I resent that!"

There was a brief pause because I was speechless, something that is out of character for me. Not that I couldn't think of anything to say, but because I was ashamed of myself. Then I said in a low voice, "You're absolutely right. And do you know something? I don't deserve your business. Now before you hang up, I want you to know that I think you have a right to be very proud of your son, Jimmy. He sounds like a fine young man, and I am sure he will make an outstanding doctor. And I sincerely appreciate what you just told me because I learned a valuable lesson. I just hope that someday you'll give me another chance."

It was two years later when he came in to see me at the dealership. "Well, Joe," he said, "I'm giving you another chance." Not only did I sell him a car, but one for his son, Jimmy, too. Incidentally, I kept my door shut that time, and I always have ever since.

Several years ago, a young saleswoman asked me to observe

her give a sales presentation to a prospect. "I must be doing something wrong, Joe," she said, "but for the life of me I can't figure what it is."

I watched her give a beautiful sales presentation; she said all the right things. Her close was smooth and her confidence level was high. Still, no sale.

"What went wrong, Joe?" she asked me. "That man needed a new car, and he could afford it, and I offered him a wonderful deal. Where did I fail?"

"Betty, you're right. You did all the right things. I think you were terrific. But you made one fatal mistake, and I'm dead sure you're not even aware of it."

"What?" she asked excitedly. "I've got to know."

"I counted six times when you looked at your watch. And each time you did, your prospect seemed to clam up a bit. He had to be thinking to himself: 'She'd rather be doing something else with her time than talking to me.' Now, if you really want to know what time it is, put a big clock on the wall so you don't have to be so obvious about it. But for heaven's sake, don't signal a message to your customer that you're in a hurry to get rid of him."

"To tell you the truth, Joe, I didn't even care about the time of day. It's just a bad habit I must have. But of course you're right. I'll never do it again."

She gave me a big hug for my advice, and a few weeks later she called to tell me she had been selling like gangbusters ever since.

HOLD ALL CALLS

Just as my door is always closed during a sales presentation, I call the main switchboard to say: "I'm in conference, so would you please be sure to hold all of my calls." Not only does this make the customer feel like a VIP, it also keeps in-coming calls from interrupting my timing. I'll guarantee you that as soon as you start talking on the telephone, the prospect will cool off. I can't imagine any salesperson taking calls during a sales presentation, yet I see this happening all the time. Did you ever see an attorney take a call while pleading a case, or a surgeon taking a phone call in the middle of an operation? Well, neither should a salesperson.

It really makes my blood pressure boil when a salesclerk takes an incoming call and says to me: "Excuse me, I'll be right with you." Then he or she talks on the telephone for several minutes. Before I storm out of there, my stock answer to these rude salespeople is: "I don't understand why you did that. I took the time to come into this store. Why are you giving that person a higher priority than you're giving me?" For the life of me, it simply doesn't make any sense how anyone can be so shortsighted as to give time to a stranger on the telephone when he or she is eyeball-to-eyeball with a customer in the flesh.

By the same token, when you're in the prospect's office, I think it's appropriate to say: "What I have to explain to you is important, so may I suggest that you tell your secretary to hold your calls?" Most people will do this when you ask them to in a courteous manner, and again, it avoids having an untimely call interrupt the sales presentation. By the way, these interruptions are equally annoying to the customer.

THE FACT-FINDING SESSION

Too many salespeople think they can control the sale by not allowing the prospect to get a word in edgewise. This school of thought actually believes sales are made by outtalking the other guy. I completely disagree for three reasons: First, questions are asked to get the necessary answers to find out what the prospect's needs are. Second, questions are a sign of sincerity, expressing a desire to help the prospect. Third, when questions are properly asked, they do, in fact, help maintain control of the sales interview.

I don't care what product you sell—automobiles, computers, houses, insurance, securities—you have to ask a lot of questions to find out what the prospect's needs are, otherwise, you'll end up working in the dark. It by no means indicates that you're giving up control by allowing the other person to speak. Nobody who really understands the art of selling can possibly think that a sales presentation is supposed to be a one-way conversation. *It's a two-way conversation,* and it's your responsibility to make the prospect feel comfortable participating in it. If you do this properly, you won't lose control, but instead, you'll gain it.

Just as a trial attorney cross-examines somebody on the witness stand, you, too, can ask questions, get responses, and maintain control during a sales interview. A real estate salesperson, for example, must do this with a prospect before dragging a husband and wife all over town showing homes that might not be of the slightest interest to them. So, prior to showing the first home, he conducts a fact-finding session in the office or perhaps on the telephone even before an appointment is set up to view homes.

"How many children do you have?" he asks. "What are their ages and do you intend to enroll them in public schools or private schools?"

"Do you own your present home?"

"What is its present value and how much equity do you have in it?"

"What price range are you interested in purchasing?"

"Do you have a preference for a particular neighborhood?"

"Do you prefer a certain style of house?"

"How many bedrooms do you want?"

"What size lot interests you?"

"How important is it to be near public transportation?"

"Do you like a one-floor or two-floor plan?"

"Have you sold your present home?"

"How soon do you have to have occupancy of a new home?"

After the realtor has asked a long series of questions, he says, "Let me do some checking to see what's on the market at this time. I have a couple of ideas that I think you might like. If so, would you be available to view some homes this afternoon?"

An hour or so later, the realtor calls back and says, "Based on what I think your needs are, I have four homes in the northeast section of town that I feel you may be interested in." He then makes arrangements for convenient times to show the homes.

Can you imagine the couple's reaction if the same salesperson said upon receiving their initial call: "Come right on over and

I'll show you some houses"? They'd think: "He hasn't the slightest idea what we want. How can he possibly serve our needs?" This would be like a doctor saying to a new patient: "Where does it hurt?" Upon being told that the pain was in the patient's stomach, the doctor would then reply: "Okay, let's cut you open and do some surgery."

I think it's a naive and serious mistake to have preconceived ideas about what customers want without first making a sincere effort to find out. In car sales it would be foolish to attempt to sell a particular model without first exploring what the individual's interests are. For instance, I wouldn't consider pushing a green two-door coupe because that's the car the dealership wanted to move that day. Nor would a furniture salesperson start off by selling a six-sectional sofa to somebody who just walked in off the street without having the slightest notion about the customer.

Asking questions is the surest way to obtain knowledge. Albert Einstein, the father of the theory of relativity, and one of the brightest scientists ever, said: "The important thing is not to stop questioning." And one of England's greatest writers and poets, Rudyard Kipling, gave us the following poem that I kept under the glass on my desk:

> *I keep six honest serving men*
> *They taught me all I knew;*
> *Their names are What and Why and When*
> *And How and Where and Who.*

Professional salespeople obtain the information they need by conducting fact-finding sessions, and as the name implies, it's a series of questions asked of prospects. The first questions should be general. For example, when I initially approach a customer, I casually introduce myself by saying, "Hi, I'm Joe Girard." And then I add, "And your name is . . ." Notice how nonthreatening I make it. By starting a sentence this way, people automatically complete it by stating their name. Some salespeople automatically start asking a series of questions, while others ask permission to do so. Either way is all right; I recommend doing what's most comfortable for you. If you ask permission, simply say: "Do you mind if I ask you a few questions to enable me to better understand your needs and how I may serve you?"

In the beginning, I recommend asking general questions. The following represent a cross-section by salespeople in different fields:

COMPUTER COMPANY REP: "Tell me about your business."
                        "What can you tell me about your present system?"
                        "What do you want your computer system to accomplish?"

INSURANCE AGENT: "Tell me about your philosophy on life insurance."
                        "Tell me about your family."
                        "Tell me about your present insurance program."

STOCKBROKER: "Tell me about your past investments."
                        "How do you feel about income-related stocks versus ones with the potential for capital gains?"
                        "What are your financial objectives?"

The purpose of these types of questions is to investigate the needs of the prospect and to get a conversation going. Of course, what he tells you will help you determine the direction of your sales presentation.

Later you can begin to ask more detailed questions to help you zero in on specifics. The following are samples of detailed questions that could follow your general questions.

COMPUTER COMPANY REP: "What kind of inventory problems do you currently have?"
                        "How long does it take to process your payroll?"

"How many workstations do you want your computer to service?"

"How many accounts do you want your system to be able to handle?"

"What is your manufacturing plant's turnover ratio?"

INSURANCE AGENT: "How did you arrive at the amount of life insurance you now carry?"

"How much in life insurance premiums do you presently pay?"

"What plans have you made for retirement?"

"Tell me about your current partnership agreement."

STOCKBROKER: "What is the size of your present portfolio?"

"What are your thoughts on tax-free municipals?"

"How do you feel about the so-called glamour stocks selling at high multiples?"

"How do you feel about buying on margin?"

"What size investment would you feel comfortable with?

In each of the above examples, the salesperson initially started out with broad topics and later zeroed in with specific questions. The initial set of questions probed and then led to more thought-provoking problems that were geared to arouse the prospect. I believe questions should be kept simple. There is no need to go overboard and attempt to impress the prospect with how much you know, or for that matter, how much he doesn't know. And avoid jargon, buzz words, and technical terms that may confuse the prospect. Speak the same language that your prospect speaks. Don't overwhelm him with how smart you are and how little he knows. Ask nonthreatening, easy-to-answer questions, and when a sensitive or personal question must be asked, preface it with an explanation about why it must be asked.

Notice how the computer salesperson inquired about the nature of the prospect's business and needs. Later, he zeroed in on questions about specific problems in need of solution. The insurance agent and stockbroker followed a similar pattern of questions. In each example, the salesperson eased into the more difficult questions *after* the prospect became an active participant in the conversation.

As I emphasized earlier, listening is a vital part of selling. Yet here in the fact-finding session, it is taken even one step further—you must make a full effort to draw the prospect into the conversation. After all, while there may be some people who feel quite at ease while talking freely, others need to be encouraged to open up. To accomplish this, you should ask "opinion questions" such as "What do *you* think about...?" "Would you agree with me that...?" "Have you ever thought about...?"

Questions of this nature require more than a yes-or-no answer and therefore invite the prospect to participate in the conversation. Once you ask a question, be certain to keep quiet long enough to give your prospect enough time to respond. I remind you that there is nothing wrong with having a pause in the conversation. Even after he finishes a sentence, I recommend that you remain silent for a moment or two—he may be reflecting before he expresses another thought.

When a fact-finding session is properly executed, you elevate yourself to a professional level considerably higher than most run-of-the-mill salespeople. You become an authoritative figure and position yourself in a consulting role rather than a selling one. By doing so, you gain control of the sale!

ACT WITH AUTHORITY

By now you should know that when I say "act with authority," I'm not suggesting that you be arrogant or stuffy. That's not my style. And if you act that way instead of controlling the sale, you'll contaminate it.

Instead, I emphasize knowing your business inside out, and it will be so obvious to others you won't have to put on a big front. Not only will you win the respect of others, but you will better control sales presentations. People simply are more respectful to salespeople who demonstrate expertise in their field.

A real estate broker, for example, doesn't have to boast that she knows her territory better than any other broker in town to demonstrate she, in fact, does. Her familiarity with the area surfaces by her actions as she drives from neighborhood to neighborhood showing homes. In a similar manner, her client recognizes that when she shows a home, she, herself, is not going through it for the first time. She has done her homework well, and it is evident. Likewise, during the point in her presentation when the subject of a mortgage is discussed, her expertise on financing assures the buyer that she will provide her professional service in the securing of a loan. She exerts her authoritativeness by *demonstrating* her knowledge; it is not something that can be faked. To act with authority, there is a price to pay. You earn it by working hard to become an astute student in all aspects of your business.

A life insurance agent must also pay his dues so that he, too, projects an air of authority when he speaks. Not only must he possess product knowledge, but today's agent must come equipped with strong legal and tax backgrounds. His competence in these areas is essential for selling life insurance products that solve problems on such matters as estate planning and partnership buy-sell agreements. Sophisticated clients, in particular, will respect his astuteness, and they will rely on his authoritativeness to guide them on what and how much insurance is needed to provide adequate coverage.

Salespeople who make regular calls on their customers can increase their sales volume when they are viewed as experts in their field. For instance, physicians depend on the expertise of medical supply representatives, and those who have won their confidence are the ones who are most likely to succeed in this industry.

I don't care what you sell, people respect expertise. In today's marketplace, everyone wants to deal with a professional. And once you're acknowledged as such, prospects will sit back and listen to what you have to say. This, I believe, is the best way to set the stage to control sales.

Have you ever noticed how some people try to pass themselves off as experts with their fancy titles? Instead of using the word "salesperson," their business cards refer to them as consultants, supervisors, advisors, and so on. With some outfits, everyone, including the brand-new sales reps, has "vice president" printed on his or her business card. Of course, a title by itself doesn't cut the mustard. While overstated credentials may get your foot in the door initially, it is just a matter of time before the prospect discovers how much or how little you know about your business.

How many times have you seen a salesperson come around a second time with his supervisor. "This is Mr. Thomas, our regional vice president, and he wants to review with you some data that you might find interesting..." It's the man-from-the-next-town-is-the-expert routine, and people are often willing to hear what Mr. Big Shot has to say. If he is all that he's built up to be, people will listen and he will in all probability take control of the sale. But if he is all title and no substance, both he and the rep are apt to receive a swift kick in the seat of the pants. And deservedly so.

WHAT TO SAY WHEN THE PROSPECT ASKS: "HOW MUCH DOES IT COST?"

No salesperson wants to be asked about the price of his product until he's good and ready to quote it. Obviously, you don't want to quote a price until you have demonstrated the product's value. Only when the prospect knows what he's getting for his money will he recognize the product is worth buying at the asked price.

For this reason, my gut reaction is to ignore the first request and continue with my presentation as if the question had never been asked. I just act as if I didn't hear the question, and I continue to sell without skipping a beat. If the prospect asks a second time, I say, "I'll get to that in a moment," and I still continue and quote the price when I think it's time to divulge it.

The third time, I say, "I'm getting to it, but I want you to know enough about what you'll get for your money so you'll realize what a good deal I'm giving you." And in a friendly way I'll add, "Now stop worrying about what it costs and listen to what you're getting."

Then, when I finally quote the price, I build up the suspense by saying, "Now I know you appreciate a good value, so I know you're going to flip when you see what a bargain this is." After a slight pause, I continue, "Okay, now for the big moment you've been waiting for. . ."

After I write down the price and hand it to him, and before he can speak, with a big smile on my face I add, "Now, didn't I say I was going to take real good care of you?" When it's put this way, people usually agree.

IT'S OKAY TO GIVE A NOW-AND-THEN NO

While you want to control the sale, you never want it to be so obvious that your customer feels uncomfortable, or even worse, resentful. With this in mind, it's perfectly fine to have to say no now and then. In fact, when I'd say, "I'm sorry but we don't have it with that feature," I have sometimes scored a few points by being up-front. Furthermore, if a prospect wanted a certain option that I didn't have, I never knocked or downplayed his reason for mentioning it. If I did, I would have insulted him by criticizing his judgment or taste. You don't make sales by putting down your customer.

By knowing when and how to say no, customers often say, "Oh, that's all right, Joe, I can live without it." But by giving them an argument, they begin to blow things out of proportion and make a minor issue a necessity.

Top negotiators know this lesson well and will often let themselves get "caught" so they're put in a position of having to throw in a few ringers as a compromise. The same holds true in selling. By letting the prospect feel as though he's won a few points, he feels good about himself and he feels relaxed. On the other hand, if you overwhelm him with the perfect yes answers every time, he starts looking for ways to get one up on you. I say let him have a few of the ones that don't matter anyway. Additionally, you'll score a few points for your truthfulness. To my way of thinking, when you say no at the right time, it helps you get the one yes you need to close the sale.

8

DIFFERENT CLOSING TECHNIQUES

"**D**idn't you ever get bored selling only cars for so many years, Joe?" people ask.

"Never," I reply, "because no two sales presentations ever are the same." In addition to having a variety of automobiles to sell, as well as the numerous new models released each year, *no two prospects are ever the same!*

I also get a thrill out of closing sales. To me, every one is different, and this is what makes selling both challenging and exciting. It is a particular high when a doubting Thomas comes in and walks out as a contented customer. Then, too, I love the instant gratification. At the end of each presentation, I know if I did my job well. When I perform well, I make X amount of dollars for my time and effort. There's nothing like working on straight commission to get the adrenaline going. At the end of each working day I also know if I had a good day or a poor one. It's so easy to keep score because all you have to do is look at the size of your commission check. And the only way commissions are earned is by closing sales.

I don't think a salesperson can do a decent job today without being armed with an arsenal of different closes to use according to what develops during the sales presentation. The days are long gone when you can get by on one close, using it on everybody! To be equipped with only one closing technique would be comparable to a featherweight boxer who knows how to throw only one kind of punch stepping into the ring with the world heavyweight champion, or a baseball pitcher who throws only fastballs. To be a winner, a major league pitcher needs several good pitches—a curve ball, a slider, an off-speed pitch— as well as a strong fastball.

Like the big leaguer who approaches the mound prepared to throw several different pitches depending on who's at bat, who's on base, what the score is, and so on, you must rely on a reserve of closes to carry you effectively during any particular sales presentation. For example, one close might work perfectly for the prospect who complains that he can't afford to buy, and another is suited for the procrastinator who wants to talk it over with his wife. Yet another is perfect for the guy who is a shopper. And if, for example, the first attempt to close someone who can't make up his mind doesn't work, I'll keep right in there pitching away until I've convinced him that he should buy today, after all. Unlike the pitcher who is limited to throwing four balls before the hitter draws a walk, I have no such rules that dictate I must stop at the fourth closing attempt.

I dread to think how poor my sales career would have been if I had sold cars with only one type of close. For the record, the majority of my sales were made *after* the first closing attempt had failed.

This chapter includes a smorgasbord of closes from which you can choose those that may be appropriate for your sales career. Perhaps you're already familiar with some of these closes be- cause I don't profess to claim each of them as my own. In fact, many closes have evolved with many salespeople making lots of changes over the years. I've added a few touches here and there, and no doubt you will, too. There are no patents or copyrights on any of them, so I recommend that you review the following closes and choose those that are best for you.

THE ASSUMPTIVE CLOSE

While Chapter 3, "Assuming the Sale," covered this subject in depth, let me remind you that this is the most commonly used close. However, its frequent usage is no reason to shy away from it. I recommend using it because it works. Don't argue with success. Frankly, I don't think a book entitled *How to Close Every Sale* possibly could be complete without strongly emphasizing the assumptive close.

Again, the assumptive close is executed by expecting the prospect to buy. To do it properly, your mind-set must be geared simply to writing up the order. Period. There is no other option, so there's no need to ask for the prospect's decision. You assumed that he or she is buying.

Perhaps the most common line used in the close of the majority of sales in America is "Do you want to pay by cash, check, or credit card?" Let's analyze this question because by understanding it, you will grasp the concept of the assumptive close.

The question could be asked by any salesperson—a travel agent, a retail clerk, an office equipment rep, etc. It ignores the possibility the prospect may not buy. Furthermore, it is not offensive. It is a simple and direct question, and there is no way the prospect can answer without consenting to buy.

One favorite feature of the assumptive close is that you can repeat it several times during a single presentation. For example, if the prospect fails to answer and instead says, "I want to shop around," you can continue selling and use this close later in the presentation. Notice how this works in the following example from a retail television store:

SALESPERSON: "Do you want to pay by cash, check, or credit card?"

CUSTOMER: "I'd like to think it over."

SALESPERSON: "I know you're going to like the remote control feature. You'll wonder how you ever got along without one before."

CUSTOMER: "I agree, but it's an option I've lived without for all these years."

SALESPERSON:	"It's not an option, it's standard equipment, so you are not paying anything extra for it. It *comes* with this model. Is the morning the best time of day to have it delivered to your house?"
CUSTOMER:	"The afternoons are better."
SALESPERSON:	(Writing up the order) "You live on . . . ?" (Notice how this is stated so the customer can automatically give his address.)

After the order is written up, the question is again asked: "Do you want to pay by cash, check, or credit card?" With this close, you assume, assume, assume.

THE ASSUMPTIVE STATEMENT-AND-QUESTION CLOSE

With this close, the prospect gets it with both barrels. As the name suggests, you make an assumptive statement and close the sale by asking an assumptive question.

INSURANCE AGENT:	"I'll use your home address for billing purposes, Tom. Now, do you want to handle this annually or semiannually?"
TRAVEL AGENT:	"I'll book you for two first-class, round-trip tickets, Phil. What auto rental company do you prefer?"
SUIT SALESPERSON:	"I definitely recommend that you buy these two dress shirts because they go perfectly with your *new* suit." (This is said before the prospect has even

> consented to buy the suit!) "Now, which
> of these three ties do you want to go
> with your suit?"

THE MINOR/MAJOR CLOSE

This closing technique resembles the assumptive close and can
be used for selling any product. It is based on the premise that
people have more trouble making major decisions than minor
ones. To conduct this close, you propose a series of easy-to-
make minor decisions, the total of which add up to a major one.

For instance, a life insurance agent would propose a major
decision by stating: "By signing your name on the application,
you are obligating yourself to pay a monthly premium of four
hundred dollars for the next twenty-five years." Can you blame
a person for wanting to sleep on that one?

To get the prospect to agree more easily, the agent may ask
the following questions instead:

> "Would you like to handle the payments monthly,
> quarterly, or annually?"
> "Is it okay to use your home address for the billing?"
> "Would you spell your wife's first name for me? You
> do want her as your beneficiary?"
> "Would you please okay this application right here
> to give us permission to check with your doctor?"
> "Put your okay on this line, too, that states all of the
> above information is true."
> "Please make out your check to the company for
> this amount right here." (The salesperson points to a
> written figure rather than saying it out loud.)

The uncomplicated nature of these minor decisions makes it
easy for anyone to buy. And by answering all the questions, the
prospect buys in a painless way. Most people are capable of
making numerous minor decisions, but ask them to make a

single major decision, and you face an entirely different situation. Your job is to ease the burden of decision making.

LITTLE MISTAKE VERSUS BIG MISTAKE

With this close, you emphasize that it's a big mistake not to buy, but under the worst possible scenario only a minor mistake to do so. This close is especially effective for selling insurance and services such as roofing, equipment repairs, and so on.

Ed Ellman, one of the nation's leading insurance agents, tells his prospects: "Alan, one way or another a decision will be made now, even if you think it best to make no decision. You may decide to invest three thousand dollars into a premium for insurance that proves unnecessary at some later point. While none of us like to make even a one-dollar mistake, your business or lifestyle will not fundamentally be altered by that sort of minor mistake. Or you may decide to take action by deferring a decision that really means doing nothing. This might save three thousand dollars . . . but it could lead to a five-hundred-thousand-dollar mistake. Tell me, how easy would it be to correct a five-hundred-thousand-dollar mistake . . . especially if it occurs at the most critical time of your business existence?"

The legendary Ben Feldman, who is perhaps the greatest life insurance agent of all time, uses the same rationale. In trying to convince a prospect to invest $20 a week into a $50,000 policy, Feldman says, "It's as though my company set up a special escrow account and put in fifty thousand dollars. As you pay premiums, money simply piles up. A business should be something to take money out of as well as put into. So I'll accumulate the cash for you—for only twenty dollars a week.

"But beyond accumulating cash for you, I'll do something else. The day you walk out, I'll walk in—and put fifty thousand dollars in the cash register *tax-free*. In your tax bracket, you would have to make over one hundred thousand dollars to equal that . . . probably have to do a million dollars in sales to duplicate it.

"Tell me, if you had another twenty dollars in your checkbook, I don't think you would feel very wealthy. If you had twenty dollars less, I doubt if you'd feel you were broke. Frankly, if you ever get to the point where twenty dollars makes that much difference, you're broke and you don't know it."[1]

In each of the above closes, the prospect is given a choice where the downside risk is so high that the decision not to buy exposes him to a maximum danger. A roofing contractor might use this same close by saying: "My company will repair your roof for twenty-seven hundred dollars. If you choose to put off this decision, you could end up with a repair bill of fifteen thousand to twenty thousand dollars, because the water damage that will eventually occur will ruin your ceiling, walls, furniture, and carpeting."

Using the same close, an auto mechanic points out: "If we don't install a new starter, in a matter of time you'll have flywheel damage, which means removing the transmission to make that repair. Then, instead of looking at a three-hundred-dollar repair bill, we're talking about a lot of extra labor that could run as much as twelve hundred dollars."

As you can see, each time this close is used, the prospect is potentially exposed to a far more serious problem by choosing not to buy.

CHOICES OF THREE

Over the years, I have discovered that the more choices presented to prospects, the more difficult it becomes for them to make up their minds. While I don't have concrete evidence backed by formal research, I have observed that when people have to choose from more than three choices, they have a hard time determining which to pick. Although I can't tell you why people become confused when four or more electives are available, I recommend offering a maximum of three.

For example, a jeweler might have a dozen diamond rings to show a customer, but after conducting a fact-finding session to determine the customer's price range, the desired cut and color, etc., he will actually show only three rings.

Likewise, a mutual fund salesperson might say following a

fact-finding session: "I recommend one of three programs for you." He then shows projections based on monthly investments of $200, $300, and $400. "Tell me, ma'am, with which of these three monthly payments would you feel most comfortable?" An estimated 50 percent of the people pick the one in the middle when offered a choice based on cost. It's as if they don't want to look cheap by selecting the least expensive, nor do they want to appear extravagant by buying the top-priced item. Of the rest, half will choose the least costly and the other half will buy the most expensive. When prospects ask "Which do most people choose?" I take it as a sign that they're being cautious, and consequently I say, "I recommend you take the one in the middle, which is by far the most popular." With this reply, I make their decision for them.

THE COMPROMISE CLOSE

When all other objections except price have been eliminated and the prospect still can't decide, I recommend making it easy by offering a compromise. The following are examples of how this works:

STOCKBROKER: "Tim, based on what you've told me, I suggest that you do not take a full position at this time. But we both agree that this investment can substantially benefit you, and as always, timing is a primary consideration. So what I'd like to do is simply this. Let's not start off with ten thousand shares, but instead let's take advantage of this investment with a minimum commitment of five thousand shares." (If a period of silence follows, the broker may continue.) "Or would you feel more comfortable starting out with three thousand shares?"

YELLOW PAGES
SALESPERSON: "I understand how tight your advertising budget is, Myrna, so rather than going with the half-page, let's go with the third-page at this time." (He can always come down to a quarter- or an eighth-page.)

INSURANCE AGENT: "Ed, I realize from your comments that you're not prepared at this time to invest in a million-dollar policy. But you do agree that you have a strong need for additional insurance, and that this is one purchase that can't wait for a convenient time. Let me recommend that we don't start with the maximum investment you'd make if you had the funds available. Instead, let's make a smaller commitment to guarantee some security for the present. Let's go with the $700,000 coverage."

With this close, half a loaf is always better than none. And more importantly, once you win over the account, you open the door to increasing it in the future. Ask any top salesperson who has used the compromise close for several years, and he or she will tell you how many large accounts started out as small orders. As the saying goes, "From little acorns grow mighty oaks."

DON'T KEEP IT A SECRET

After having exhausted all other avenues in a long session with a difficult customer, I've said, "Look, Jerry, I won't keep it a secret. I want your business." You'd be surprised how effective it is to come straight out and say this.

If this still doesn't get the sale, I'll say, "What do I have to do to get your business?" Then I go into my routine about asking the prospect if he wants me to get down on my hands and knees and beg for his business. But for those of you who don't feel comfortable about getting down on your hands and knees to make a sale—and I can understand how most salespeople are too inhibited to do this—*never be too proud to let people know how much you would appreciate their business*.

THE BEN FRANKLIN CLOSE

If Ben Franklin used this technique, you know it's an old one. It's been used in the insurance field for years, and it's so effective that I know it works in all industries. Here's how it goes:

> "One of my favorite great Americans is Benjamin Franklin. I'm sure you'll agree with me that he was one of the wisest men in our nation's history. Do you know what old Ben did whenever he confronted a difficult situation such as you're facing right now? He'd get out a plain sheet of white paper and draw a line right down the middle. Just like this"—you must talk and write at the same time—"Franklin would write 'Yes' on this side of the page and 'No' on this side. Then he'd list all the reasons favoring the decision in the Yes column, and he'd put down anything that was against it in the No column.
>
> "What do you say we do the same thing? Okay, now let's think of everything we could to put down under 'Yes' . . ."
>
> A life insurance agent, for example, would list such things as the low premiums today versus waiting until tomorrow; the benefits the policy pays; the applicant's present insurability, which could change at any time; the high cash value; etc. Then the agent would say to the prospect, "Now, you tell me what you think should go in the No column."

* * *

When this close is properly executed, items in the Yes column far outnumber those in the No column. Of course, no salesperson with an ounce of common sense would volunteer to give the negative reasons the prospect shouldn't buy.

SOLVE THE PROBLEM, DON'T CREATE A SECOND PROBLEM

Your job as a salesperson is to solve problems. But when you don't close the sale after demonstrating the need, you actually create another problem. When this happens, I recommend that you make an issue of the problem you created by saying, "It's rather amusing, Mark, but do you realize what has happened during the course of the past hour? When I came into your office, our conversation was initiated because you had a problem. Now you have a second problem because you have to get rid of me. You can solve the second problem simply by asking me to leave. And if you do, I'll be on my way. But that won't solve your first problem, will it? So I suggest that we spend a few more minutes together and see if we can solve that problem, too."

Another version of this close is: "Mark, I'm sure you realize that I didn't come here to create a problem for you. I came to solve a problem. I know how busy you are, and although you certainly were aware of your existing dilemma before I entered your office, I realize that you felt comfortable putting it on hold and ignoring it. But as we both know, problems of this nature don't go away by inaction. If you fail to acknowledge your problem, it's only going to compound itself.

"So, even though you mightn't be too happy with me at the moment because I caused your problem to resurface, I know that once we solve it, I will have performed a fine service for you and you're going to be grateful to me for it. With this, I strongly urge you to bite the bullet and let's get this show on the road . . ."

THE SELL-IT-WITH-LOVE CLOSE

I've used this close many times on husbands and wives, parents and children—it worked anytime a family member was buying a car for a loved one. Picture a scenario in which someone is accompanying another person for whom the first person is going to make a purchase. For instance, a father and a daughter are shopping for her college graduation present—a new car. At a crucial point during the close, I lay a guilt trip on the father that puts him in a position where he's embarrassed not to buy the car. "You know something, Susan?" I say. "You're a very lucky young woman."

"Why do you say that, Mr. Girard?"

"To have such a wonderful father," I say in a soft, melodramatic tone. "I would have loved to have a father like yours when I was young. I hope you appreciate your daddy buying you such a beautiful car."

"Oh, I really do."

If this doesn't make poor papa melt, I don't know what will. I've actually seen some tough, hard-hat types get tears in their eyes with this one. However, I've always said it with sincerity. I do wish my father would have expressed his love for me in such a generous way, and I certainly admire other fathers who are like this with their children.

A life insurance agent once made a strong pitch to my wife and me at our kitchen table. June was against it because the premium was too high. But he made the sale in spite of her objections when he said, "You know, I've seen a lot of wives complain that their husbands were spending too much money on life insurance." Then he paused. My wife nodded her head in agreement, and then he added, "But I've never seen a widow complain, Mr. Girard."

When he saw how emotional his comment made me, he called over to my small son and daughter. "Hey, kids, I want you to stop with your homework for a minute and come over here." Little Joey and Gracie came to the table and the agent said, "You know, your pa really loves you. He's quite a guy."

With that, the agent didn't say a word and started writing down information on the application. The four of us had tears in our eyes; our love for each other filled the room. The agent then took control of the conversation by adding, "Okay, kids, it's time to go back to your homework," and he closed the sale without a trace of resistance from my wife.

Another time June had me accompany her on a visit to a furrier. As a buyer, I was no match for the woman who showed us coats. She had my wife trying on coat after coat. Finally, June found one she especially liked, and she must have spent ten minutes admiring herself in the mirror. "I just love it, but I know it's far too much money, honey."

Before I could open my mouth, the saleswoman said, "You look like a dream in that coat. Don't you agree, Mr. Girard?"

"Er, yes," I mumbled with my eye on the price tag. I then added, "June, you look magnificent."

The saleswoman then said to June, "You'd be amazed how many husbands come in here with their wives and tell them how fat they look in fur. Honey, you are a lucky woman to have such a caring and thoughtful husband. I bet he doesn't deny you a thing."

That woman made me feel as if I were nine feet tall. I was beaming all over. Then it dawned on me. I had just bought my wife an expensive fur coat!

Dwight Lankford, with Piedmont Marketing, Inc., is perhaps America's top salesperson in the time-sharing recreational real estate industry. He, too, closes sales by appealing to the executive-type prospect's love of his family. "A profile of my typical customer is a guy who is work obsessive, what you'd call a workaholic," Lankford says. "Consequently, he has guilt feelings about not spending time with his family. I zero in on this and emphasize, 'By buying a time-sharing unit, you make a commitment to take the family on a vacation every year, and most importantly, it's quality time. You can either use your own unit, or as a family, go through our catalog and select a vacation in some exotic location in a thousand different places.'

"Nine out of ten times, the wife is for it because she wants her husband to make the commitment to spend quality time with the family. So if the man resists, a strong sense of urgency is automatically created by pointing out that by virtue of the fact that he's not willing to say yes, he's unwilling to set aside a specific time for the family every year. 'If you don't say go for it now,' I say, 'you never will. When was the last time the family took a really quality vacation? It's a shame your beautiful family has to miss these years together, that once gone, can never be replaced. You really need to lock yourself into a definite vacation every year, and this is the ideal way to do it.'" As you can see, Lankford makes a strong emotional appeal to buy today—if not, the customer's family will be denied what they are entitled to receive.

THE FOLLOW-THE-LEADER CLOSE

This close is based on the theory that there are more followers in this world than leaders. Therefore, some prospects will buy only after they know that prominent people have signed up. How will you know when some name-dropping is in order? The obvious signal is when the prospect asks, "Who else in the area have you previously sold?"

Another subtle, silent, but meaningful signal is the status symbols you may observe. For instance, a woman wearing a blouse with a designer label, a designer watch, designer sunglasses, and carrying a designer handbag is somebody who is willing to pay several dollars more for a sense of identity. Men are just as likely to be decorated with status symbols. For instance, they might have little alligators and polo players on their shirts, jackets, belts, and ties, and they own their share of expensive items that serve as status symbols with name brands, such as Rolex watches. When historian, jurist, and Pulitzer Prize–winner and Librarian of Congress emeritus Daniel J. Boorstin in an interview with *Forbes* magazine was asked why someone is willing to pay extra for a Pierre Cardin product, he replied that the buyer is "counting on the fact that you're going to be impressed I bought it. Maybe it's worth something to tell others that I've got the money, the taste, and prestige hunger to buy a PC frying pan."[2]

There are dozens of status symbols in homes and offices that tell you the prospect is influenced by how other people think—

and to me, these clearly indicate that it's in order to start dropping as many names as you can come up with. Some salespeople carry long lists of customers to use for this purpose, while others go a step further. They show off endorsement letters written by satisfied customers.

Endorsement letters are quite effective, especially those that rave about the fine service you and your company gave. Sometimes you have to solicit these letters. While satisfied customers may think highly of you, few will write about it without some coaxing from you. As a matter of fact, I used to keep a stack of letters in my desk to show customers. Some were unsolicited, while others were from happy customers whom I requested to write. For instance, when a customer would make a comment such as "I've never been treated so royally from a salesman, Joe," I'd say, "How would you like to do me a big favor?" Then I'd explain how much I'd appreciate it if he would put it in writing.

People are strongly influenced by the knowledge that you have sold to prominent members in the community. As I stated earlier, procrastination comes from the fear of making a poor decision, so a client's mental gymnastics might be: "Those people are bright and astute, so if they bought, I'm sure it must be a good value." Dropping the names of some of the leading citizens in the area also does wonders in showing that you are a legitimate salesperson—this is especially true when you make a cold call and sense that the prospect's uncertainty is based on a lack of familiarity with you or your company. Some people's rationale is that if they do get taken, at least they'll be in good company!

THE HARD-TO-GET-IT CLOSE

If you can remember your first crush on the cute little girl or boy who played hard to get back in grade school, you will readily understand how this close works. It's a fact that people want those objects that are not readily available. If diamonds were as common as pebbles, people wouldn't bother to pick them up off the ground. Hard-to-get items are desirable because not everybody can have them. It boils down to greed and ego.

This human nature is the basis of the hard-to-get close. This closing technique confronts buyers with the question of "Can you qualify?" rather than "Do you want to buy it?" When properly executed, prospects forget their concern about making a poor buying decision—their mind-set becomes fixed on if they'll be able to buy at all!

To get a clear picture of how this works, let me take you back to World War II when goods were extremely scarce. It was a seller's market, and customers were willing to buy the largest available quantities at top prices. Consequently, salespeople displayed enormous independence; of course their confidence was based on knowing they would sell every last piece of merchandise in their limited inventories. In the automobile business, for example, a salesperson was doing somebody a favor when he'd simply move a favored customer's name up on the list so he could buy a car, even though it carried a high premium over the sticker price. The same was true with practically everything.

Leading salespeople use this technique today even in times of a buyer's market—and when properly carried out, it still works like a charm. Why? Because it's based on the same human nature that made Adam and Eve desire the forbidden fruit. *People want those things they can't have.* And the harder it is to get those things, the more people want to have them. Use this form of reverse psychology in your sales presentation, and you will realize substantial gains in your success ratio.

The following are examples of how the hard-to-get close works in the sale of practically any product:

INSURANCE AGENT: "Fred, I'll level with you. Your health background is doubtful. I have some serious reservations that you'll qualify for this policy. Now sign your name on this line giving the company permission to contact your doctors, and I'll set up an appointment for your examination." This close works because every insurance agent knows that people who are uninsurable want as much life insurance as they can get! It's not that the need is greater for unhealthy people; they want what they might not be able to get!

CAR SALESPERSON:

"Tom, I think you should consider the less expensive model. I don't think you're ready to buy the top-of-the-line." Here, the customer is challenged and wants to prove that he is financially capable of buying the most expensive car available.

FURNITURE MANUFACTURING REP:

"My company only wants one dealer in this town"—in a bigger city, "area of town"—"to represent our line of furniture. Frankly, Jay, we want the strongest, most prestigious retailer, and I'm not sure your store is the right one." Again the customer is challenged to prove that he is eligible to do business with the company.

ART DEALER:

"This rare painting is a collector's item, and I want to see it owned only by someone whom I consider a serious art collector. To be quite frank, sir, I simply won't sell it to somebody who doesn't appreciate it. I'm not interested in selling it to somebody whose only qualification is that he can afford to pay the price of the painting. A qualified buyer must be an individual of fine tastes,

a true lover of high-quality art."
Here, too, the buyer must prove
himself worthy of buying the seller's product.

REAL ESTATE AGENT: "This may be too much house for
you. Perhaps I should show you
some smaller homes in another
neighborhood where you'd feel more
comfortable." Here, the agent sub-
tly challenges the prospect and puts
him on the defensive.

In each of the above incidences, the salesperson's strategy is
to make the prospect prove his or her worth as a buyer. This
close works because it appeals to people's greed and to their
egos. People want what others can't have, and they want to be
accepted. If it wasn't for these human characteristics, exclusive
country clubs would have difficulty attracting members. To
paraphrase one of America's greatest wits, Groucho Marx, I
wouldn't want to join any country club that would have me for a
member.

THE SALES MANAGER'S CLOSE

This is a close that every sales manager can use when accompanying a trainee. After the sales trainee's presentation is over
and no sale has been made, the sales manager says, "Do you
mind if I make a comment before we leave?"

"Not at all," the prospect says.

"As you know, I'm Jeff's sales manager, and I've been quietly
observing his sales presentation. I think he did a fine job. What
do you think, Chuck?"

"I agree. I think that once he's had some seasoning, Jeff will
be one of your best salespeople."

"I think you'll also agree that Jeff is a truly low-pressure
salesman."

"Yes, I do agree," the prospect says, nodding.

"As a matter of fact, he was so low pressure that he didn't

even try to get your order today. Please correct me if I'm wrong, but you *are* interested in buying our product."

"I'm certainly going to think about it."

"Well, speaking strictly as an observer, I know you want it, and I know something else, too. Jeff certainly wants you to own it. Isn't that right, Jeff?"

"Absolutely."

"So what I suggest is that you fill out the order form, Jeff," the sales manager says while he places the form and pen in the salesperson's hands, "and start filling out the information you need to complete your sale."

If the sales trainee doesn't pick up the ball from here and run with it, he isn't ever going to make the grade!

IT AIN'T NECESSARILY NO

I'm sure you've heard the one about the diplomat who means maybe when he says yes. When he says maybe, he means no. And when he says no, he's no longer a diplomat.

By the same token, a salesperson should never take no to mean a sale can't be closed. What I like about having a reserve of closes available is that if you don't succeed with the first, you can try and try again until you do finally close the sale.

As I always say, after I get seven nos I start to think, "Maybe he isn't going to buy. I'll try just three more."

9

CREATING A SENSE OF URGENCY

To succeed in sales, you must provide your prospect with a concrete reason he or she should buy your product today. If you fail to do so, your prospect will have no incentive to buy immediately and will postpone making a decision. Simply creating a need for your product is not enough, unless the prospect will suffer dire consequences by not owning your product as soon as possible. A lifeboat salesman, for example, would have had no trouble convincing the captain of the sinking *Titanic* to buy his wares without delay.

It is rarely possible, however, for a salesperson to have the good fortune to appear on the scene at the exact time of certain disaster. For this reason, products such as liability insurance, seat belts, and fire extinguishers must be sold in anticipation of a future need. A sense of urgency has to be created before the emergency, not after the fact. I believe it is possible to incite people to feel an urgent life-and-death desire to own any product. When you can inspire your prospects to feel such a need to buy your product, your closing ratio is bound to soar.

THE LIMITED OFFER

It's hard to imagine not running into the limited-offer close during the course of a day. You see it all the time in newspaper and television advertisements, and department stores and supermarkets use it to peddle everything from mattresses to frozen orange juice. For example, a retailer makes an offer that's good for a limited period. Failure to buy within a certain time frame means that you lose the opportunity to get a good deal. Limited offers work, and this explains why the American public is constantly bombarded with such inducements.

You, too, can create a sense of urgency when selling eyeball-to-eyeball with your prospects. It's a matter of arousing the buyer with the concern that his or her indecision will result in a lost opportunity.

The limited offer can be used in practically every sales situation, from the two-for-one soap sale to the limited partnership real estate deal. One of the best I've seen in a long time was an ingenious incentive from Airstream, Inc., a company I consider to be the Rolls-Royce of recreational vehicles. A couple of years ago, Board Chairman Wade Thompson and President Larry Huttle put together a package that offered a $15,000 savings bond to people who bought Airstream's top-of-the-line model. The bond, available for a limited time only, was especially appealing to elderly couples who felt guilty about spending so much money on a luxury motor home. Knowing the bond would ultimately someday go to their grandchildren eased the guilt.

While $15,000 would be available in ten years when the bond matured, the discounted cost of the $15,000 bond was only $3,800, an affordable incentive for Airstream. A $3,800 discount is no big deal on anything in the $80,000 price range. And a lump sum of $15,000 in ten years had incredible sizzle and created a powerful urgency to buy before the offer expired.

BUY BEFORE THE PRICE INCREASES

In the automobile business, prices were constantly increasing so I frequently used this as an incentive to close sales. "We're expecting a rise in the sticker price on this model on the first of the month," I'd say at the end of the month, "so I recommend that you take advantage of this price today." Of course, I'd say this to somebody only when a price increase had been announced and was certain to occur. It's foolish for a salesperson to misrepresent anything because it will come back to haunt him.

A stockbroker can effectively create a sense of urgency by saying, "Tony, I'm calling you today because this appears to be an excellent time to buy General Products. I feel it's important for us to accumulate these shares at forty or less. At this price the shares are selling below six times earnings. Do you realize that this is an extraordinary value for a blue chip company with such an outstanding record? Let's take advantage of this opportunity. I recommend that we accumulate three thousand shares at this price." In the investment field, a delay in making a decision can be costly, particularly in a bullish market.

A life insurance agent can tell his prospect that the rates will go up as the prospect's age increases. "Eddie, your birthday is right around the corner, so I want to submit your application today to take advantage of the lower premium." If the prospect's birthday is a month away, the agent might say, "It usually takes four to six weeks for the application to be processed. I'll do everything in my power to speed it up so we can get the policy issued *before* your birthday."

A clothing manufacturer's rep says, "We're anticipating another increase in the price of fabrics, so I want to submit your order for these suits in time for the merchandise to be delivered at the lower prices." As long as there's inflation, the possibility of price increases exists and serves as a motivation for making buying decisions today.

THE CLOCK-IS-ALWAYS-RUNNING CLOSE

Airstream's president, Larry Huttle, explains that with many of the people who buy a product such as a recreational vehicle, a race against the clock takes place. Here, the clock he refers to is old age. "An RV is what I consider something to have fun with. After all, nobody *has* to own one. Florida is understandably one of our biggest markets where the customers are elderly, and with these people, our salespeople create a sense of urgency by pointing out that they have made sacrifices all of their lives, and now is the time to start living a little. 'Why put off buying an RV when you can afford it now?' an Airstream salesman stresses. 'Buy it while you still have time to enjoy it. Don't wait until it's too late. If you're ever going to do something, I recommend that you do it now. Right this minute. We both know you deserve to own one, and I don't want you to walk out of here denying yourself something that you know and I know you're entitled to own.'"

I know personally how persuasive this sales pitch is. Larry Huttle is the guy who convinced me to buy an Airstream (I'm now in my fourth one and loving it). After talking to Huttle, I knew that if I didn't buy one on the spot, I never would! Yeah, I'm the first to admit he created a sense of urgency, and he was so right. I'm not getting any younger! Had he not been so persistent I would never have bought, and I would have lost out on one of my greatest pleasures.

Every salesperson has a clock of one kind or another. It's your job to demonstrate that there's a race against it, and the more that clock ticks down, the more your prospect loses. A good computer salesperson points out that without a new system, the poor efficiency of the old system will cut into the prospect's profits. A manufacturer's rep emphasizes how many sales are lost by a retailer who does not carry the company's line. A real estate agent stresses how much more the prospect pays by renting rather than owning a particular property.

Television evangelist Oral Roberts, whom I consider one of the greatest salespersons in America, understands how the race against the clock can motivate people to part with their money. When Roberts told the nation that if he failed to raise $8 million by the end of March 1987, "God will call me home," it got the attention of his flock. During the last week of the month when he still needed $1.3 million to reach his death-preventing money goal, an owner of two Florida dog-racing tracks was sufficiently inspired to donate that precise amount, thereby winning a reprieve for the Oklahoma preacher. Still, Roberts let the clock run. He went on a fast, secluded in his Prayer Tower, and asked his flock for still more cash, which continued to pour in.

As you can see, the race against the clock works with selling anything from freezers to religion. It just takes a little imagination to tailor-make this close to sell your product.

SELLING ONE-OF-A-KIND PRODUCTS

Selling a unique product or one that is not readily available creates a sense of urgency when it's time to close the sale. A salesperson is in good shape if he or she has a one-of-a-kind product to sell, and situations of this kind actually are more common than many realize. For example, a real estate agent might have an exclusive listing on a house. If you want that particular house during the time of the listing, it is not possible to buy it unless you deal with that agent! So in effect, a monopoly exists on that individual house.

When we purchased our home, it was love at first sight. The realtor recognized how much June and I loved it and said, "The owners of this home have had it on the market for six months, and they're most anxious to sell it. Their original asking price was too high, but they've dropped the price to where I *know* it will sell within a matter of days. I know you want it, so I suggest putting in a bid immediately. I showed it to another couple this morning, and they asked me to show it to them with her brother this evening. I'm sure they're going to make an offer. And two other realtors are showing it later this afternoon."

To this day, I don't know if the agent was on the level with us, but June and I didn't want to take any chances and lose what we thought was our dream house. We signed the contract immediately. Our decision making was sped up by our concern that we might lose the opportunity if we stalled.

Real estate agents can also lease space in commercial properties such as office buildings, apartment complexes, warehouses, and shopping centers using the same technique as the residential realtor. Jennifer Becker, a top salesperson for the M. H. Hausman Co., regional shopping center developer in Cleveland, Ohio, tells a prospect, "We had a ninety-nine point two percent occupancy rate in our Lansing, Michigan, Meridian Mall for the past six years. We only have vacancy because we are creating it.

Some of the original tenants' leases are expiring, and we are choosing not to renew their leases so we can bring in more upscale retailers. There are several other retailers who have expressed strong interest in this particular space, so if you are interested, I recommend that you act quickly before it is no longer available."

This close works well in service-related industries, too. For example, a custom-home builder might tell a prospect he sensed was eager to move into a completed house: "My schedule is fully booked from June until next March. This is April seventh, and if I start construction by the eighteenth of this month, I'll be able to work your home into my schedule. Of course, if you prefer to wait until next spring, that's okay with me." Notice the subtle pressure put on the buyer. Computer sales reps, office equipment salespeople, and heavy machinery salespeople can also use this technique effectively by stating: "Our delivery and installation schedule is booked for fourteen weeks, but it just so happens I had a cancellation, so if you want, I could put your order in its place and have it delivered and installed next Tuesday."

Franchise sales reps often close sales by saying, "My company is interested in only one dealer in this area, and to date we have six interested parties. If you're really as excited about this opportunity as you claim to be, I recommend that you sign the contract today. And if you do, I'll do my best to use my influence to help you get the territory. But as much as I'd like to, I can't guarantee you anything."

When I sold cars and would sense that the buyer was chomping at the bit to own one but was somewhat hesitant about making up his or her mind, I'd say, "This is the only one we have in inventory in this color and with all the options you want. Now, I can have it prepped and you can drive it out of here by early this evening. But if you choose to wait, I think this one will move out of here quickly. We sold two just like it this morning. Now, there's always a chance I could call some of the other agencies and locate one for you, but that could take as much as a week, and I can't promise that you'll get it with the exact equipment you want." I'll pause for a few moments to let the prospect sweat a little, and then I add, "Why don't you do yourself a favor and just say yes, and I'll tell the service department to get it ready for you to drive out this evening?"

Airline ticket agents are notorious for selling tickets by letting the passenger know that if he doesn't act quickly, there's a risk of getting closed out because the flight is about to become fully booked. This seems to work especially well—particularly on businesspeople such as me who work on airtight schedules, skipping across the country like some people drive across town. For instance, a few days ago I called to ask about a flight to Toronto and was told, "We have only two seats left on that flight, Mr. Girard, so if you want it, I advise you to book it immediately." While I wasn't certain I wanted to take the early flight, I was concerned about losing it because I had to be in Toronto that afternoon, so I confirmed the reservation. As you can see, whenever a limited number of a product is available, it's possible to create a sense of urgency. You don't have to sell rare one-of-a-kind art to make a limited offer to your prospect!

SELLING TO THE HIGHEST BIDDER

When a group of buyers are pitted against one another at an auction, a wonderful environment exists in which the seller offers his or her product to the highest bidder. I've attended auctions where the goods sold included fine art, antiques, distressed merchandise, horses, cattle, and bankruptcy and estate liquidations. From a salesperson's viewpoint, this is an ideal way to create a sense of urgency because buyers are forced to make instant buying decisions. If you've ever heard a professional auctioneer talk at a hundred-mile-a-minute speed, you understand how quickly bidders must respond. And all it takes is a split-second signal, the raising of one's arm or the pulling on one's ear, to be the highest bidder—and congratulations, you are now the proud owner of a _____.

A real estate broker might, for instance, obtain a listing on a desirable home, one that she thinks will sell quickly, and create a bidding war for it. To accomplish this, she shows the home to ten prospects during the first two days it's on the market, informing them that they have twenty-four hours to submit a bid. She sets a bottom price to begin the bidding, on the present homeowner's approval, then sells the house to the highest bidder.

TIMING IS EVERYTHING

Every business person understands the importance of timing, so I recommend using this as a strong selling point to create a sense of urgency. You don't have to sell real estate to say, "Alan, I'm sure you understand the expression 'Timing is everything' in business. And I'm sure you'll agree that you would feel terrible today if you passed up buying your house. Isn't this true?"

Before you use this line about buying a house, you should investigate to find out when your prospect purchased his or her home. If it's been a while, take into consideration how the cost of real estate has increased during the past decade, then point out the large amount of appreciation in the home over the years. If the prospect does not own a home, you can point out certain well-known real estate properties that have skyrocketed in your community, or how substantial gains would have been realized had he or she purchased the stock of a particular well-known local company at such and such a time. Or you might say, "Imagine if you would have bought a McDonald's franchise way back when." Or how about, "I have a friend who sold every stock in his portfolio in early October 1987." Every businessperson recognizes the good fortune in knowing when to buy and when to sell.

10
THE DANGERS OF OVERSELLING

There's a story about a devout Catholic mother who is anxious to marry off her thirty-five-year-old daughter but is upset that her daughter's fiancé is a Protestant. "He's a nice man, but you must convince him to convert to Catholicism," she preached to her daughter. "Insist that he go to Mass with you, then have the priest talk to him."

"Yes, Mama," she replied obediently.

Several months later, the daughter came home with tears in her eyes and bawled, "The marriage is off."

"What happened?" wailed the mother. "Everything was going so well. I thought you had him sold on becoming a good Catholic."

"Yes, but I did such a good job on selling him that now he's decided to become a priest."

The moral of the story: *Never oversell!*

Overselling is one of the major reasons why sales that should have been closed go by the wayside. Too many salespeople are so busy talking up a storm that they talk their prospect out of the sale. That's right. They sell the guy, and then they buy back what they sold him! Again, I urge you to be a good listener—and have the good sense to know when to shut up! Diarrhea of the mouth is a disease known for shortening the life of many sales careers.

FEAR OF REJECTION

I believe the number one reason a salesperson oversells is his or her fear of rejection. It doesn't take a genius to recognize when a prospect is sold on the product, and I give the average salesperson credit for knowing that. Sadly, the guy is just too scared to close the sale because he doesn't want to ruin a relationship that he perceives has blossomed into a beautiful friendship.

The typical salesperson is under the false impression that by attempting to close the sale, the prospect will be put on the spot and will say no or—even worse—become offended by what could be interpreted as high-pressure selling tactics. So rather than risk facing the moment of truth, the salesperson continues to sell when he should shut up.

Overselling is self-defeating because it undermines what otherwise would have been an effective sales presentation. The salesperson's lack of confidence is contagious, and the prospect soon becomes leery and suspicious of making a buying decision. His mental gymnastics is: "Why does this person continue to sell me when I already want to buy? There must be something he's trying to cover up." As a result, the more the salesperson sells, the smaller his chances of closing.

DON'T CONFUSE YOUR CUSTOMERS WITH UNNECESSARY DETAILS

For starters, you don't have to present every fact you know about your product to sell it. Likewise, it isn't necessary for your prospect to become an expert on it before he can make a buying decision. The way some people sell, they must think it's mandatory to explain every detail of their product—and by gosh, they refuse to let anyone buy until they do! I've witnessed salespeople go through their complete sales presentation, make an attempt to close the sale, and before the prospect could say, "Yes, I want to buy," they went into windy explanations of trivial facts that created total havoc. Talk about overkill!

Then there are others who think a sales presentation isn't complete until they've sufficiently impressed a prospect with their vast product knowledge. They oversell until their prospects are bored to tears. These salespeople walk away feeling superior, but with empty order pads.

Both types talk their way out of more sales than they close. Imagine, for example, a computer salesperson bombarding a prospect with a lot of technical jargon about bits and bytes. People who buy computer products want solutions to problems— they're interested in the application of the machine, not detailed explanations about a technology that enables the computer to switch information at a microsecond rate. Too much technical information doesn't win customers, but it does dilute the selling effort.

I'm not suggesting that you shouldn't be an expert in your business. You should. No field is so complicated that a salesperson should be excused from knowing his or her business backward and forward. But you must execute good judgment and know how much information to give which prospects. With this in mind, a computer sales rep should emphasize different selling points to an engineer than to a chief financial officer. Of course, keep in mind that there are always exceptions. Some seemingly unlikely prospects are interested in technical details, and if so, you must be prepared to fill them in on the information they request.

Believe it or not, I've witnessed automobile salesmen who routinely refused to open the hood to discuss the mechanical aspects of a car with a woman. Today, many women are quite knowledgeable about technology, and it's an insult when a salesperson deletes information he would have presented to a man. However, some prospects—men as well as women—have no interest in or understanding about gear ratios, horsepower, or catalytic converters. Not only is it unnecessary to show what's under the hood to every customer, it can be counterproductive. You must size up your prospects and custom-make your sales presentations to their interests.

In some cases a salesperson is legally obligated to disclose specific information about his product. Examples are the selling of shares in a limited real estate partnership, and the offering of a high-risk, newly issued security. Once again, I recommend using good judgment in how much and what information you give to close the sale. While I am not suggesting that you withhold important details, I advise you to close the sale when you feel it is appropriate instead of presenting more confusing and unnecessary facts that are of no interest to the prospect. Later, after you have secured an order, you can say, "Oh, by the way, let me explain something I feel is important for you to know," and then fill the buyer in on the necessary details.

SILENCE IS GOLDEN

When you ask for the order and a period of silence follows, don't feel obligated to say something for the sake of conversation. Give your prospect enough time to think about the decision, and don't interrupt his or her train of thought. As I mentioned earlier, some people have the false impression that silence represents a flaw. Not only is it permissible to have a long, silent pause, but in my opinion, it's a welcome relief.

A lull in a sales presentation usually seems much longer than it actually is. It reminds me of the feeling one gets after being put on hold on the telephone. It's as if time stands still. Seconds seem like minutes. In an eyeball-to-eyeball sales presentation, the silence is deadening and it's natural to give into the temptation to break the silence. While the expression "He who speaks first loses" suggests that if the customer speaks first he loses, I think people who make good buying decisions are winners. On the other hand, if you, the salesperson, speak first, you risk losing the sale. So you must remain quiet until your prospect speaks first. And yes, the silence may border on maddening. No matter, you must discipline yourself to remain silent.

"HAVE YOU SOLD YOURSELF YET?"

An effective close is to simply say to the prospect, "Have you sold yourself yet, or should I continue to tell you more?" If you're told that it's necessary to go on, then simply comply with this request until you feel it's time to try to close again. On the other hand, if you get a positive reply, then close the sale no matter where you are in your presentation. You can always explain some of the selling features of your product later. Never feel as though you're obligated to discuss everything about your product *before* your close. It's okay to save some extra goodies to throw in as a bonus after you get the order. The important thing, however, is that you don't want to disturb the flow of your presentation and miss a closing opportunity.

Like other closes I have mentioned throughout this book, you can use this technique more than once during a sales presentation. To do so, you simply repeat: *"Now* have you sold yourself, or do you want me to tell you more?"

The following are a few alternatives to saying "Have you sold yourself yet?"

AUTOMOBILE SALESMAN:	"Isn't this the perfect model for you?"
CLOTHING SALESWOMAN:	"I think this dress is exactly what you have been looking for. Don't you agree?"
REAL ESTATE BROKER:	"This is *the* house for your family. Do you agree or should we continue to look at other homes?"
INSURANCE AGENT:	"Is there anything else you need to know before you sign the application?"

Notice that in each instance, when the prospect makes an affirmative statement, the sale is closed. If he resists, the salesperson simply continues to give him more reasons to buy and attempts to close the sale once again. Obviously when the above questions are asked, the salesperson feels as though he has given a full presentation, so my advice is to avoid spending too much time between your "Have I sold you yet?" closes.

11

GOING ALL OR NOTHING

I believe in working with the odds, and the only time I'm willing to buck the percentages is on a trip to Vegas. The casinos are in business to make money, and because of their high overhead, they must make sure everything is stacked heavily in their favor. So I go there to have fun, and once I lose a certain amount of money at the tables, I chalk it up to the cost of entertainment and call it quits. I go knowing the odds are against me, and I accept it for what it is.

Anyone who plays against the odds on a day-to-day basis, however, is doomed to be a loser the majority of the time. As the expression goes, "Even a blind pig will stumble on some corn now and then." But smart people work the percentages. In Vegas, they're the guys who own and operate the casinos. They have winning down to an exact science, and with such large numbers of bettors each day, it's almost mathematically impossible for the casino operators to lose. Although selling is not an exact science, you, too, must understand the odds.

The odds to which I am referring have to do with your closing ratio—the percentage of closes made with each first attempt versus those made during callbacks. Here, you must address the question: Will your sales volume be greater if you call back on indecisive prospects, or will you generate more business by going all or nothing and attempting to close every sale on the spot?

Without addressing ethical implications, I do whatever generates the best bottom line for Joe Girard. And my bottom line is directly related to the percentage of sales I close. If you're not interested in your bottom line, there's no point in getting out of bed to go to work each morning. I always felt that the name of the game was to make as much money as I possibly could during the time I work. I don't understand how anyone can dispute me on this score. Yet those salespeople who ignore the odds are doing just that—they're willing to accept less money for their time and effort. How anyone can agree to having a large chunk taken out of his or her paycheck is beyond me!

THE CALLBACK CLUB

It's been said that a sale is made every time a sales presentation is made. Either you sell the prospect, or he sells you. The prospects who sell you are members of what I refer to as the Callback Club, a nonexclusive club with countless members who say they'll call back after thinking it over. Or for those of you who work in a retail store, you're told they'll be back. (I call those members of the Be-Back Club.)

Every time you allow a prospect to join the club, you set yourself up for disappointment. If you had been more persistent, you would have had a better chance of closing the sale. I've seen salespeople accumulate dozens of promised "sure" sales that never happened. Some go as far as to convince themselves that they actually earned the commissions on these sales while waiting for the calls. It's only a matter of time before they must face disappointment and discouragement.

I remember a young rookie salesman who, over a three-month period, accumulated eighty-four prospects who promised to buy cars by the middle of December. "I'm going to sell more cars than Girard," he boasted, "even if only half of those who promised to buy do, in fact, buy." He was so convinced that he was going to rewrite the record books that he spent a small fortune on Christmas gifts for his wife and three young children. Sadly, only three of the eighty-four prospects actually bought cars, and it had the poor guy talking to himself.

"I don't understand it," he cried on my shoulder. "It makes me lose faith in my fellow human beings. How could people lie to me like that?"

"People are sincere when they say they're going to call back," I explained. "But a lot of other things distract them. Don't forget, they had their Christmas shopping to do, and they have their share of monthly bills and unexpected expenses, just like we all do. You know the old saying 'Out of sight, out of mind.' But perhaps you learned a lesson from this experience. And if you did, then your present disappointment has been worth its weight in gold." The young salesman claimed that he did, and I said that in the long run, he'd more than make up for those lost sales. I also explained that if he had hung in there by being persistent, he might have closed between 60 and 70 percent of the ones that got away.

It's bad enough to forfeit sales because you weren't persistent, but there's another loss—the wasted time and effort exerted in contacting callbacks, time that could have been spent more productively by calling on good prospects!

After all, when you get right down to the nitty-gritty, the most valuable thing a salesperson has is his or her time. I don't know about you, but I place a high value on mine, and I don't like to waste it. Each day I walked into the showroom to sell cars meant I had to get out of bed that morning. I'll tell you something: I like to sleep. I mean it—I can sleep like you wouldn't believe. So, one of the things I did when I got up each morning and looked in the mirror was to say out loud: "Somebody is going to pay for getting me out of bed!" Sure, I was giving myself a pep talk to get myself motivated, but the truth is, I didn't want anyone wasting my valuable time. What's more, knowing that callbacks were worthless, I viewed each prospect as a deer hunter looks at his prey. A hunter only gets one shot at a deer, and if he misses, that's the last he'll ever see of that deer. The same applies to prospects who say they're going to call back. With this in mind, my advice is to give them your best shot when they're hot! And the time when they're red-hot is when they're eyeball-to-eyeball with you! If you let them get away then, you've lost them!

THE LAW OF DIMINISHING RETURNS

I believe it's vital for every salesperson to have a clear understanding of an important law, one that is not enforceable by any court, but one that nevertheless is essential to obey. It's *the law of diminishing returns*. Perhaps you already know it, but I'll explain it anyway with what I call my apple-eating analogy: A young boy with a large appetite is given a juicy red apple, which he quickly devours with immense pleasure. He is given a second apple, which he also enjoys, but not quite as much as the one he just ate. Having no more hunger pains, he is given yet another apple, which he eats reluctantly, and from which he derives no particular enjoyment. Having had his share of apples, he is ordered to eat still another one, which he does slowly, becoming sicker and sicker with each bite. The pleasure he derives diminishes with each apple.

In the sales field, the law of diminishing returns works in the same way. At the end of your presentation, you are in the best position to close the sale because all of the facts about your product are most clearly understood. What's more, this is when your prospect feels the strongest need for your product. By the following day, two things will have happened: The prospect will have forgotten some of your product's finer points, and his enthusiasm will have diminished. And each additional day that passes, his need and desire to own your product will have continued to decrease. And while his memory is slipping, he is thinking less and less about how your product will benefit him. Soon he's thinking about how his money could better be spent somewhere else. What this translates into is: *The greater the lapse of time, the less chance you have of closing the sale*. The prospect cools off.

Once you realize that your chances of making a sale decrease as time goes by, you'll recognize the value of giving every close your best shot while your prospect is still hot. Any salesperson worth his salt understands how these odds work in his favor, and he is smart enough to risk applying high pressure to make or break the sale.

What you sell and how well you sell it will change how high pressure affects your closing ratio. It is true that there will always be a small number of Callback Club members who would have bought in a day or two had you applied no pressure, but you have to write them off in exchange for the greater number you'll get by going all or nothing. Keep in mind that you must be consistent. You can't give in to the temptation of making exceptions and letting people off the hook. Over a period of time, I guarantee that your persistence will pay off.

One more thing about the Callback Club—don't be so proud that you won't let another salesperson try to sell someone you couldn't close. Often, when one salesperson can't make the sale, another might take over and do something a little different and have better success. I used to tell the other salespeople in my dealership that before they let a prospect walk, they should let me have a crack at closing him. I would then be introduced as the sales manager, sales executive, whatever. I'd give them twenty dollars for each customer turned over to me. After I "bought" the customer, the salespeople got paid their twenty bucks no matter what happened. After all, half a loaf is better than none. Unfortunately, some of the salesmen were "too proud" to turn sales over to me. They resented seeing me make a large commission while they only got twenty dollars. So, while they saved face, they lost money.

A prospect can be turned over to somebody else in any field. For example, a copier salesperson can say he wants to introduce the customer to his manager, who is authorized to make a special deal. A life insurance agent can say he's bringing out an expert who specializes in retirement plans.

"I'M SORRY BUT I DON'T MAKE CALLBACKS"

Once you understand the law of diminishing returns, if you're smart, you won't make callbacks. And there's nothing wrong with being up front with people and telling them you don't. It's easy. All you have to do is say, "I'm sorry, but I don't make callbacks." If anyone should happen to ask you why, simply explain to them that it's bad business. "I can't afford to spend my time calling people who should have bought from me at the time of my presentation. This is the best time to make your buying decision, Mr. Prospect, before you become confused or forget the reasons you should buy today." People will respect you for your sincerity and, for the most part, will react favorably when you say this. You can follow it up by saying, "Now, let me give you some more reasons you should make a decision today," and continue with your presentation.

Remember Dwight Lankford with Piedmont Marketing, the expert on selling recreational time-sharing properties? Lankford's experiences with callbacks indicate that only 2 percent ever buy. Yet when he goes all or nothing, his chances of closing the sale run as much as twenty times higher. Knowing that the odds are so greatly stacked against converting a callback into a sale, Piedmont Marketing lets all prospects know that they have to buy on the spot or forget the deal. To drive this point home, prospects are told they will receive a first-day discount (depending upon the property, the discount can be $800 to $1,500, a sizable discount considering that the average one-week time-sharing sale is about $7,500).

"My salespeople know that *nobody* gets the discount the next day. There are no exceptions to the rule. Never! If we prostitute this rule just one time, then we make everyone a liar. Let's suppose a prospect came back the next day with a check in his hand for the discounted price, and I say, 'Sure, I'll sell it to you for the same price as yesterday.' If this were to happen just one time, then none of our salespeople would ever have any conviction in the first-day discount, and everyone who ever received it would be made a fool."

Lankford explains, "If a prospect asks why we have this rule, we tell them, 'History has taught us that when people leave, less than two percent of them return, so we simply have the first-day discount as an incentive to help them make a decision.' By being so direct with people, they know we mean what we say."

NO SINGLE PROSPECT WILL
MAKE OR BREAK YOU

There was a time in my career when I needed money so badly that I desperately had to make the commissions on every sale. In the beginning, I lived from paycheck to paycheck, and the food put on my table each week, the house payments, and the car payments depended directly on my sales production. It hurt badly when I'd lose a sale.

But in time, I could afford to let prospects walk out without buying, and no longer did I become physically ill when they didn't buy. While I don't remember the exact sales presentation when I felt so at ease, it was an important milestone in my career. Its significance was that I realized that no single prospect could make or break me. While this may not seem like a big deal to you, it was to me because I never again would *sell scared*. I finally had the security to know that I could risk losing sales and not be badly hurt. I could afford to put the needed pressure on those people who said they'd be back when they decided to buy a car—and I'd no longer be afraid that I'd blow the sale by doing so. Even so, I never lost my motivation or hunger, or what some people refer to as a salesperson's "killer instinct." Believe me, my desire to close every sale remained intact.

In most sales careers, no single prospect is so important that if you don't get his or her business, you will go bankrupt. A life insurance agent can lose a sale, and there are numerous other prospects to call on. When a stockbroker strikes out, he simply has to dial somebody else. Real estate agents also have endless numbers of prospects.

I realize that there are some industries in which a salesperson has a given number of accounts, and if a major one is lost, the consequences are severe. For example, an appliance manufacturer's rep may have a large retail chain in his or her territory that generates a major portion of his total business. In this case, losing this one account can even cost the rep his job.

An account executive with an advertising firm may have only one client. While these are exceptions, I acknowledge that these situations exist. Those sales careers are "ulcer jobs," and I don't envy anyone who has to rely so heavily on one customer to make a living. If you happen to have a job of this nature, you better give such incredibly outstanding service that it's unthinkable for anyone even to consider doing business elsewhere. I'll discuss how to do just that in Chapter 13, "The Sale Begins *After* the Sale." For now, I will say that I don't believe in putting all your eggs in one basket, but if you must, you had better guard that basket with everything you've got!

GOING FOR THE BIG ORDERS

Always remember that you sell to make money—there's no disgrace in earning big commissions. With this in mind, it's important to generate orders large enough to make your work worthwhile. I'll cushion this remark by mentioning that it is sometimes necessary to open a new account with a minimal order. As I previously mentioned, mighty oaks grow from little acorns.

However, simply getting a token order isn't necessarily always good for business. Sometimes a small sale means that the customer doesn't consider your product and company significant enough to warrant a bigger order, and unless you're able to increase it, your business will be treated accordingly. A good example would be a food wholesaler who introduces an off-brand soft drink to be marketed through large supermarket chains. If only a few cartons are displayed on the shelves among the many dozens of major brands, the new product will probably get buried and will quickly be dropped. So sometimes simply getting a foot in the door with a token order backfires and becomes the kiss of death, closing the door for future business.

Another case in point would be a wholesaler who sells merchandise to exclusive retailers in a specific area. For example, a particular line of office furniture might be carried by only one dealer in a small community with a population of 25,000. With three office-furniture retailers in the area, a manufacturer's rep doesn't want to open up a single account that carries only a small inventory of his line. The rep must establish a certain quota with which he feels comfortable. Otherwise he should do business with one of the other two retailers.

Some manufacturer's reps view small orders as total defeat. Not only do they receive a next-to-nothing commission, but the buyer is relieved after he sells the one or two units he bought. Or worse, the merchandise collects dust because the buyer has little incentive to put a sales effort behind it. Then on your next call, the buyer complains, "Don't sell me anything else. I couldn't do anything with what you forced me to buy the last time." So not only do you make little commission, but you receive a lot of aggravation to boot.

Now, back to the impractical economic reasons for writing up small orders. Sometimes it's wise to have an all-or-nothing attitude and go for a large order even if it means risking losing the sale altogether. In practice, there is only a slight risk compared to the excellent chance you have in landing the larger order. Besides, rarely will you lose the initial sale. For instance, in the automobile business, after a commitment was made to buy a particular model at a rock-bottom price, I'd attempt to sell a few options to increase the size of an otherwise slim commission. In most cases, I'd turn the stripped-down car into a large sale, and I honestly can't remember ever losing a customer for trying, although not everybody went for the more-equipped versions.

I've turned small sales into big sales countless times, and more than once, I am sure, an alert salesperson has applied the same technique when selling me. It happened to me once after I had selected a twenty-dollar tie at Harry Kosins, a fine men's clothing store in the Detroit suburbs. As I pulled out my credit card to pay for the tie, the salesman asked, "What are you planning to wear with that tie?"

"It goes great with my navy-blue suit," I replied.

"Boy, I have a beautiful tie for a navy-blue suit!" With that, he whipped out two more ties at twenty-five dollars each.

"Yeah, I see what you mean. They're beauties," I said, nodding my head with approval to ring them up.

"How about some new shirts to go with these ties?"

"I could use a couple of white ones, but I couldn't find any over in that area," I replied, pointing to another counter.

"That's because you were looking in the wrong place. What size do you wear?"

As quickly as I could say sixteen, thirty-three, he placed four white shirts on the counter at forty dollars each. "Feel this fabric, Joe. Doesn't that feel good?"

"Okay, I'll buy some shirts. But I only want three of them."

See what happened? The salesman turned a $20 tie sale into a $190 sale. That's nine and a half times more than what I originally bought. Did I object? Absolutely not. I walked out as a satisfied customer. Incidentally, it's no wonder Harry Kosins does more business per square foot than any other men's clothing store in America. No wonder.

Ed Ellman, one of the nation's top life insurance agents, frequently will have two policies issued instead of the one the client applied for. "One business owner recently bought a $300,000 policy and I delivered two $300,000 policies," Ellman says, "and I told him, 'Since you passed your physical examination with flying colors, I asked a friend of mine in the underwriting department to go ahead and issue a second policy while you're still in good health. Of course, you're under no obligation to take it, but I think you definitely should.' He bought it, and the extra work I put into the second policy was virtually effortless. I generated an extra eight thousand dollars in commissions in a matter of minutes. I make several additional sales every year with this technique, and rarely does anyone seem to be offended even when he or she doesn't buy the second policy. Even when somebody resents having me bring back two policies, the occasional slack is well worth the many extra sales I pick up." Here too, when properly executed, the sale of the second policy isn't perceived as pressure, but instead as providing a service.

IN THE BEST INTEREST OF THE CUSTOMER

While lesser salespeople may think that applying high pressure is unappreciated by customers, I have a different opinion.

Personally, I think it's in their best interest, and you're doing them a disservice when you back off rather than exerting some force at the close of the sale.

Sure, I know that nobody wants to be high-pressured into buying something. Well, people may say that, but deep down, many of them have great difficulty in making up their minds. I think they *want* a salesperson to convince them to get off dead center. What's more, if a salesperson doesn't give them that needed extra push, they'll never make a buying decision. When I help people who can't make up their minds to buy cars, I feel as though I'm performing a wonderful service. I've come to the rescue of a procrastinator who is terribly frustrated by indecision. Do you remember the Aesop fable about Buridan's Ass? That's the one where the donkey starved to death between two stacks of hay because he was unable to decide which was the most desirable. I won't allow any of my customers to suffer the frustration of indecision. In my opinion, this is one of the real services that professional salespeople provide.

A real estate broker, for instance, shows a particular house to a young couple unable to make up their minds. "We've been shopping for years," the wife says, "and this is definitely what we've been waiting for. We'll sleep on it for a few days and get back with you."

The broker knows two facts that justify applying some pressure for the benefit of his clients. First, he knows the people have outgrown their present home and truly need to move soon so their children can be enrolled in time for the new school year. Second, he knows that some other brokers have been showing the house, and there is definite interest. With this information, he insists, "While I don't want to appear as though I am rushing your decision making, I strongly urge you to submit an offer today. You're not going to find a more ideal home for your family in this price range and in this neighborhood, and I don't want you to lose out. Other brokers have been showing this home, so if you want it, you must act decisively."

While some people may accuse the above broker of being high-pressure, that's not the way I see it. I consider him to be thoughtful, caring, and doing what is certainly in the best interest of his clients. Imagine how they would feel if he failed to guide their decision making at this crucial point of the sales presentation, and as a result, they lost their dream house! You must always remember that your job as a salesperson is to do what's right for your client—and this frequently includes a touch of friendly persuasion, and when necessary, some strong persuasion.

Finally, I want to emphasize that a fine line exists between using high-pressure selling and closing a sale with finesse and diplomacy. As I mentioned earlier, it's imperative to sell yourself, and while your customers don't have to love you, they must not view you as offensive and rude. With this in mind, you must be firm and confident—and don't back off from exerting some pressure when it's necessary. When you sincerely have conviction in your product and in your company, and always act in the best interests of your customers, I believe they will feel comfortable with your forcefulness in guiding them to make buying decisions. In my opinion, this is professional selling at its best.

12

HOW TO HANDLE BUYER'S REMORSE

There probably isn't a person alive who hasn't had buyer's remorse at one time or another. I'm sure everyone has had second thoughts after making an impulsive, extravagant, or ridiculous purchase.

In our fast-moving society, with today's high cost of living, we often make snap decisions only to wonder later if we acted too hastily. After all, there are so many needs and so many luxury items from which to select, and few of us have enough wealth to buy everything. With this in mind, it is only natural to think, "Should I have bought this, or would my money have been better spent on something else?"

Usually when a person buys a product, he or she does so with little or no planning. In my business, prospects may have toyed with the idea of shopping around at a few dealerships, but rarely had they actually intended to buy a car on the day they moseyed into the showroom. Top salespeople understand that many people buy impulsively—and if you can't close these sales, your sales career is going to be rough sledding. You can't limit your sales production to only those individuals who know exactly what they want and who have the determination to buy, come hell or high water. Unfortunately, these customers are not the norm. Keeping this in mind, it's natural that many customers will be consumed with doubts after they have spent their hard-earned cash.

You must be aware of your customer's mind-set and potential remorse. You must never forget: *A canceled order is not a sale!* As you well know, a lot of time and effort goes into setting up appointments and making sales presentations. With this in mind, it's a pity to lose a sale after you've won it. But people do cool off—if you let them cool off. When you lose a customer due to buyer's remorse, not only is it money out of your pocket, but even worse, it whittles away at your positive mental attitude. A canceled sale hurts considerably more than no sale!

Having created an awareness of the dangers of buyer's remorse, I will now explain in detail what you can do to overcome it before its ugly head is raised. But before I begin, I want to make sure you don't get the impression that when a sale is properly executed, I am suggesting that customers will bulk with dissatisfaction. When salespeople demonstrate conviction in their product and company, and show a sincere desire to serve customers, only under unusual circumstances are canceled orders likely to occur. On the contrary, most customers realize that you have helped them find a solution to their problems, and they are indebted for the peace of mind you have provided. While this scenario is ideal, I firmly believe it is attainable when you do your job properly.

However, as every salesperson knows, selling isn't always smooth sailing, and many obstacles unexpectedly arise along the way. For this reason, this chapter is intended to serve as a precautionary measure to eliminate potentially predictable buyer's remorse *before it occurs*. Because, although your percentage of canceled sales may be low, any canceled sale is one too many.

THANK YOU!

When is the last time a salesperson told you how much he or she appreciated your business? Or for that matter, even bothered to say "Thank you"?

It's a sad commentary, but most salespeople don't make any effort whatsoever to express their gratitude. It's as if they think they've got a monopoly on their customers. I never sold a car that an identical or similar model wasn't available from another dealership. But when somebody bought a car from me, he or she was also buying Joe Girard. I knew that, and believe me, I was thankful for the business—and I saw no reason to keep it a secret. I never made a sale in my life after which I failed to say, with total sincerity, "Thank you, and I want you to know how much I appreciate your business. I promise I'll do everything in my power to give you the best possible service to prove that you made the right choice in buying from me."

After that thought sank in, I'd continue, "Sam, I want you to know one other thing. I'll never let you down. I really appreciate that you bought from me. And believe me, by God, if you ever need me, even if you see a dozen people surrounding me, I'm going to drop what I am doing and you're going to get service like you wouldn't believe. And I'll tell you something else. I bet you'll never buy a car from anybody else again."

You see, I continued to sell because I wanted the customer to know that he or she had made a good buying decision. I didn't want anyone to feel that once the sale was made, I felt it was "in the bag," would drop him like a hot potato, and be off and running to sell somebody else. When customers feel your only motivation is to sell to them to make a quick commission, they feel used and abused. No wonder they cool off. Can you blame them?

A courteous thank-you should be automatic with every sale. I don't think you can thank customers too much. No matter how repetitious you may think it sounds, every time you do it, you reaffirm that his buying decision was a good one. I always made it a point to write a personal letter each night to every customer I sold to that day. My typical letter went like this:

May 12

Dear Mary Jane:

Just a brief note to thank you for your business and to congratulate you on your fine new car. I am sure you will enjoy owning it.

Again, please don't hesitate to call me anytime, because when you buy a car from me, you're also buying Joe Girard! I look forward to serving you for many years.

Sincerely,
Joe Girard

Larry Huttle, president of Airstream, Inc., goes even one step further. He explains, "Our salespeople call the customer the morning after the sale in addition to sending a thank-you note. And with someone they think was a particularly tough sale, they know that all they have to do is ask, and I will personally call the customer. I introduce myself as the president of the company, and the first thing I say is how we appreciate their business. I'll also ask them what they thought of our service and if they have any questions or problems they'd like to discuss with me. I give them my number to call me directly if they ever have a problem. You can't believe what a tremendous effect my call has on them. After all, when did you ever get a call from the president of a company to see if you were satisfied with the product?"

CONGRATULATIONS!

"You made an excellent decision, Susan, and are to be congratulated," a car salesperson says with a warm smile. "I know you will love driving your new car."

"Congratulations for your fine decision, Jim," a jewelry salesperson says with a hearty handshake. "You selected a magnificent diamond. I want you to know that you are getting an outstanding value, and your wife will be elated."

"I congratulate you, sir," says a computer rep, "and I assure you that you will never regret your decision to install our computer system. It will revolutionize your business."

"It's a pleasure to do business with a man who has the foresight to provide for his loved ones," a life insurance agent says. "I admire your wisdom to recognize the value of estate planning. It takes an intelligent man to plan for his loved ones' financial future, sir."

Barbara Singer, a successful account executive for *Chicago Life,* says, "Selling advertising is different from other products because, in the short run, it's difficult for buyers to recognize how much value they receive. So, for good reason, many first-time customers become hesitant after the sale. Knowing this, I always congratulate them for their wise buying decision after the commitment has been made to buy space in our magazine, and then I emphasize that the two best times to advertise are, 'number one, when business is bad, and number two, when business is good.' Although I generally say something to this effect during my sales presentation, I stress it once more *after* the sale to make new customers feel comfortable with their buying decision. They need this sort of reassurance, so I don't mind repeating something I have said before."

Always, I repeat, *always* tell your prospect that he or she made a wonderful decision to buy. Again, many buyers are nervous and have second thoughts about whether they have bitten off more than they can chew. They need to be assured that they didn't. *So tell them.*

I've been asked, "But isn't it self-serving for the salesperson to congratulate the customer?" Yes, but so what! Do it. I routinely congratulated people, and I can tell you that not a single customer ever complained. More often than not, I'd hear them sigh with relief as if to say, "Whew, I really needed that reassurance, Joe. I just spent a lot of money, and I was wondering if I had done the right thing."

I don't think I ever met a person who didn't like praise. And that's exactly what you give customers when you congratulate them on their smart buying decision. So don't keep it a secret. Tell them how wise they are for buying your product. People need this reinforcement, so give it to them.

YOU SURE ARE LUCKY...

When my kids, Joey and Gracie, were little, I bought a set of encyclopedias from a salesman who visited our home. I remember how good he made me feel. "Your daddy just bought you the best gift in the world," he said to my children, "and someday when you're older, you will really appreciate it." He made me feel as if I were nine feet tall. "What a nice man," I thought to myself. It wasn't until he was out the door that I realized how much I had spent, and then I began having second thoughts about whether I had made a smart purchase. Then I took one look at my children and I knew there was no way in the world I could even think about changing my mind. What would I tell them? I learned a good lesson that night, one that has paid for those books many times over.

Whenever I'd sell somebody who was accompanied by the person for whom he or she was buying a car, I'd make it a point to say, "You sure are lucky to have such a wonderful father, Margie. He must really love you to buy a car for you."

I'd say this when a customer bought a car for his or her spouse, mother, lover, whomever. By emphasizing this point, how in the world is the customer ever going to be able to change his or her mind and renege! After I'm through building the customer up to be so wonderful, he or she would never be able to save face!

DON'T TAKE THE MONEY AND RUN

I don't think anything arouses more suspicion in a buyer's mind than when, as quickly as the ink dries on a new customer's freshly written check, a salesperson is on his way out the door. When this happens, people become overwhelmed with doubts about their buying decision. This behavior conveys a message that your single objective is to take the money and run. It justifies what many people already think: "Salespeople are always available to sell you, but once you buy from them, that's the last time you'll see them. They're never around when you really need them." When these thoughts surface, people become resentful, and worse, anxious to cancel their order!

Yet some salespeople think that the sooner they're out of the customer's office, the better. Their thinking is based on the belief that the customer might change his mind and ask for his money back *while they're still there!* The opposite, in fact, is true. By flying out of there like a bat out of hell, the salesperson arouses suspicions that he might be hiding something. I suspect the expression "fly-by-night salesman" may have come from this behavior.

After you get the order, there's no need to make a beeline

toward the door. You just established a new customer, and possibly a new friend, so stick around for a few minutes and reassure him that he means more to you than just a fat commission check. Let him know that you care about him as a human being. No matter how many people I had waiting to see me, I'd make small talk with my customer so he'd know my interests in him weren't strictly monetary. Even when a customer was in a hurry, I'd say, "What's the rush? Do you have to run out of here so fast?" Then I'd ask him a question or two about something completely unrelated to the sale.

Just as I sell myself to new prospects before the sales presentation, I do it again *after* the sale. Doing this has a dual purpose: first, it reduces buyer's remorse, and second, it helps to generate a lot of referrals.

"ONE THING ABOUT ME, I'M NOT HIGH PRESSURE!"

There have been times when I knew it would take high pressure to close a certain sale, and for the benefit of both of us, I let my prospect have it with both barrels. I also knew that some of these customers would cool off if I didn't make the extra effort to solidify the sale afterward. With these people, I worked doubly hard to avoid having buyer's remorse cost me the sale.

With people such as this, I'd say in a soft voice, "You know, Jack, I'm sure you observed one thing about me that's different from a lot of other salespeople."

"What's that, Joe?"

"I don't believe in using high-pressure tactics. I've seen some salespeople pressure customers into buying like you wouldn't believe. But me, I couldn't sell like that if my life depended on it. I'm glad I don't have to make my living like those guys." Then I'd pause briefly before adding, "With people like you who recognize a terrific value, it's not necessary to resort to those tactics. Besides, with a deal like you just got, I feel more like an order-taker than a salesperson. Now, you do appreciate everything I've done for you, don't you?"

"Yeah, I really do, Joe. Thanks a million," prospects often would respond.

GET YOUR NEW CUSTOMER INVOLVED IMMEDIATELY

The sooner a new customer assumes ownership, the less chance there is for buyer's remorse to set in. Knowing this, I liked to get customers driving a new car home as quickly as humanly possible. If that meant having the service department prep a car so the new owner could have it that same day, that's what I'd do.

After you close the sale by creating a strong sense of urgency, it's natural for the customer to want immediate possession. And whenever possible, I recommend giving it to him, especially when you suspect the customer may cool off.

A computer salesperson could use this technique effectively by saying, "Do you mind if I put in a call to our service department, Sam? I want to set up a definite delivery and installation at the earliest possible date."

Perhaps while still in the client's office, a good life insurance agent will set up an examination for his client. As Ben Feldman comments, "The interview succeeds or fails on my ability to get my man examined. Regardless of what a man says against life insurance, if I can get him examined, I have found that seven times out of ten, he will take it. Get him examined, and it's three-quarters sold. I can also promise you this: If you don't get him examined, you'll *never* get it (the policy) sold."[1]

Here's how Feldman schedules the examination: "Surely, you can't object to an examination that will cost you nothing and that will not obligate you in any way. Let the doctor check you up, and let me see if I can get it (the coverage) for you. The company may not be willing to take you. Let's find out first . . ."[2]

A stockbroker places the order while the buyer is on the telephone so the deal is completed before the receivers are laid back in their cradles. In such instantly transacted sales via computer, there is little time for customers to get buyer's remorse.

If there is one particular industry where customers get

buyer's remorse, I'd have to say that the recreational time-sharing business ranks way up there. I've heard that its cancellation rate runs between 15 to 18 percent. Last year, friends of mine, whom I'll call Sue and Charlie, spent a "free" weekend at a newly developed resort located in upper Michigan. Their free weekend cost them $16,000 for a two-week time-sharing package they ended up buying. Their salesman was good. Real good! The next day he took them for a speedboat ride around the lake and played a round of golf with Charlie while Sue played tennis. What he did was to instill some pride of ownership in them. "This is *your* golf course," he told them, "and this is *your* lake."

To reduce buyer's remorse, the salesman took it a step further. He asked them for names of relatives and friends, and as an inducement, he offered to give Sue and Charlie small gifts such as payments of future maintenance fees, green fees, and so on. This is where I came into the picture. The same night they bought, I, as one of the names given to the salesman, received a call and was invited to spend a free weekend at the resort. Of course, he mentioned that Sue and Charlie had recommended me. By his calling their family and friends, Sue and Charlie would have felt foolish had they later cooled off. Just imagine how embarrassing it would have been for them to tell their friends that although they had recommended it to them, they, themselves, had changed their minds. I love this technique and think it works in all fields.

QUICK FOLLOW-UP

Even satisfied customers can develop severe cases of buyer's remorse if you fail to perform as promised. Nothing amazes me more than thoughtless salespeople who lose otherwise good sales because they're too busy trying to drum up new business to follow up on the details of completed sales. Ultimately they neglect their new accounts, as well.

It doesn't take much for brand-new customers to become filled with second thoughts. Sometimes it takes only a small oversight, such as forgetting to drop off a brochure, not returning a telephone call, or just forgetting to fulfill service. On the surface these details seem insignificant, but they're not to the customer. Generally, it's an item that gets blown up out of proportion that ends in a canceled sale. Then the salesperson cusses out the customer and blames him for being a hothead. The cold facts, however, indicate that the same salesperson always seems to get more than his or her share of hotheads. According to this salesperson, buyer's remorse is never his or her fault.

It doesn't matter what you sell, you should make a special effort to keep in touch with your new customers to reassure them that you were sincere when you promised to provide outstanding service. In addition to sending thank-you letters immediately after the sale, you should phone them or, when possible, stop in to see them a day or two later. For instance, a life insurance agent might contact a new client to mention, "I want to remind you about your two P.M. appointment Friday with Dr. Silver for your examination." A real estate agent calls to say, "Here are the names of three local loan officers you should see about obtaining a good mortgage." A stockbroker calls a client to tell him: "You bought 1,000 shares of XYZ Company at 21¼ and 2,000 shares at 21½."

You must keep in constant touch with your customers. And be sure to call them to relay the bad news as well as the good. Too often, salespeople shy away from their customers when something goes wrong, and this is a serious blunder. A good stockbroker, for example, calls to say: "Gary, XYZ Company was off two points today. The market was down thirty-two, but you're in it for the long run, so I don't think today's loss is anything to be too concerned about." A manufacturer's rep calls a retailer and says, "I spoke to our factory today, and we're running two weeks behind because of a temporary shortage in our materials. However, I'll do whatever I can to speed up your order."

The vast majority of customers are understanding, and they realize that certain things are beyond the control of either you or your company. They appreciate hearing from you, and they welcome your frankness. It's when you fail to communicate problems that sales fall by the wayside.

THE GREATEST QUESTION THAT SOLIDIFIES SALES

I am going to give you a question to ask new customers that does wonders to eliminate buyer's remorse. After the order is signed, sealed, and ready for delivery, and my customer is on his way out the door, I ask, "Charlie, before you go, I'd like to ask you a question."

"Sure, what is it, Joe?"

"I'm always trying to improve myself, Charlie, so there's something I'd like to know before you leave," I say with sincere humility. "You mentioned how you shopped around at two other dealerships, yet you didn't buy from them. Why did you buy a car from me instead of from one of them?"

Then I shut up and listen. I'm going to hear how much the guy loves me, and the more reasons he gives for buying from me, the more he convinces himself that he made a wise decision. He's being sold all over again—this time by himself. By repeating, in his own words, why he bought, the customer forms a clear and concise understanding about your product and why you deserve his business. He'll tell me such things as: "I bought from you, Joe, because you really care about me." "You didn't high-pressure me." "You didn't try to sell me more than I could afford." "You're a real pro, Joe." I love asking a prospect why he bought because I know I'm going to receive a lot of praise. It's also a good ego trip, but that's okay. We all need to be reinforced by hearing good things. After all, who can't use a little pep talk in the middle of the day?

As an extra benefit, every time a customer tells me why he bought from me and not from somebody else, I learn more and more about selling. It's an amazing thing, but the longer I'm in sales, the more I keep learning.

Now how in the world can he or she want to cancel, or get buyer's remorse, after telling me how much they loved me? You try this, and I'll guarantee you will hardly ever have buyer's remorse or cancellations.

13

THE SALE BEGINS AFTER THE SALE

Perhaps you're thinking that this chapter's title sounds like a play on words. I'm sure it's confusing to some people that servicing customers is even addressed in a book about closing sales. To me, however, nothing could be further from the truth—*excellence in servicing customers has everything to do with closing sales—"future sales."*

Getting the initial order is just the beginning. Today's business world has no place for anyone who drops out of the picture after the sale. Outstanding service is part of the selling effort, and anyone who fails to recognize its importance is doomed to fail. As IBM's Buck Rodgers explains, "The two words *sell-install* always go together. You can't have one without the other. Nothing is sold until it's properly installed, and nothing is installed until it's properly sold." Of course, Rodgers could have just as easily said *sell-service*, which every salesperson must always remember whether he sells computers, automobiles, life insurance, securities, *any product*, the message is always the same.

Dedication to providing outstanding service cannot be a whim, and it cannot be something that is extended only to a select group of customers. Every customer, no matter how affluent, is entitled to the best possible service. "The customer is king" must be a continuous motto for every salesperson. Nowhere is this maxim more widespread than in Japan, where salespeople refer to the customer as "Kami-sama," meaning God. And accordingly, each customer is treated with the greatest respect. I don't really believe the Japanese are better business-people than Americans, but they definitely are more service-oriented because they have to be to survive in their fiercely competitive homeland. Of course, not every Japanese company excels in servicing its customers, but those that don't, generally fall by the wayside. And it is only the most efficient service-driven Japanese companies that enter the American marketplace. It's no wonder that these companies do so well in the U.S.

The difference is not in the product itself. What ultimately assures success is the quality of service rendered. The payoff comes with repeat business and referrals by satisfied customers. It's a fact that after two years in sales, if you provide outstand-ing service, 80 percent of all of your sales for the rest of your career will result from existing customers. On the other hand, anyone who fails to provide good service will never realize the building process that comes with establishing a solid base of customers and the fine reputation that ensues. Each step that a no-service salesperson takes forward will be followed by at least two steps backward.

The long-range forecast for salespeople who are not service-driven is filled with gloom and doom. Their futures are des-tined to be glutted with frustration and disappointment. They are that vast army of salespeople who inevitably will pound the pavement, day in and day out throughout their careers, barely eking out a living. These are the salespeople who never build a solid base of customers; they find themselves starting over each year as if they had just entered the sales field. Most of them never survive in sales; they eventually burn out. So for good reason, giving your best, all-out effort to service customers is not an alternative but is vital for your survival as a salesperson. Anything less is unthinkable.

A SALESPERSON'S BELIEF TO LIVE BY

IBM has three basic corporate beliefs that govern all significant company decisions. They are (1) respect for the individual; (2)

provide the best customer service of any company in the world; and (3) expect superior performance from employees.

I have been told that these three beliefs govern every policy made by IBM management. I think it's wonderful that the IBM Corporation has achieved such immense success and, at the same time, has never compromised its integrity. While all three of these beliefs are admirable, it is IBM's second belief that I will address in this chapter. I feel it is so important that it should be tattooed on the brain of every salesperson as a constant reminder of the importance of service. It's interesting to note that this principle doesn't limit itself to customer service in the United States, or to the computer industry. I repeat: IBM is driven to provide *the best customer service of any company in the world!*

Just as a well-managed corporation has a set of beliefs by which it is guided, so must you as an individual. And your set of beliefs should be so strong that it influences your daily sales activities. While I have no intention of telling you about what you should believe, I do think that if you want to be a successful salesperson, you must be committed to providing outstanding service to your customers. I strongly urge you to adopt this belief and to live by it each day throughout your sales career, and never deviate from it. Once you commit yourself to this, you will be on your way to enjoying immense success.

REPRESENT A COMPANY THAT IS COMMITTED TO SERVICING ITS CUSTOMERS

To some degree, a salesperson is limited to the servicing commitment that his or her company is willing to make to customers. In fact, I don't think it's possible for a service-driven salesperson to succeed representing a company that is not similarly driven.

This is particularly true when technology is a major aspect of a particular product. In such cases, it is essential for service to be built into the manufacturing process, which frequently requires a steep up-front investment by the company. Products such as heavy machinery, computers, and automobiles must be produced with a certain level of quality. Fine quality, in turn, eventually means savings to the customer both in dollars and in the grief brought on by future repairs. Companies that try to save money by stripping down quality do so at the expense of their customers. When this happens, the service that you, as a salesperson, can extend is greatly restricted because it is frequently beyond your control. As a consequence, you are unable to properly satisfy your customers, and *your* integrity is put on the line.

When young people seeking a sales career come to me for advice about how to select the right company, I always stress the importance of working for a service-oriented organization. I suggest that they find out how a company services its customers *after* the sale. For example, does it send out questionnaires to new customers to generate mailing lists, and does it seek information that will help it to improve the quality of its products and subsequent service? Also, check into what kind of recognition the people in the service department receive. Companies that score high marks in this area have award programs for their service people as well as their sales force. Also, do the service department people work daily with the salesperson? When the sales department is far away from the service department—in another building, on another side of town, or in a different city—communication between the two divisions often deteriorates. There are even some companies that don't have any service departments at all or at best, provide their customers with a WATS line number, which, in turn, gives the names of local dealers that may have service departments. Not only do I tell salespeople to stay away from these companies, but I urge consumers to boycott their products.

It's too bad, but some companies put everything into their sales effort at the expense of servicing existing customers. There has to be a balance because little is accomplished when new business doesn't stay on the books. If you happen to be working for an organization that is unwilling to do backbends for your customers, my advice is to run—not walk—to a company that is strong in this vital area. You shouldn't think of yourself as being disloyal for making the switch; any company that lacks the willingness to serve its customers doesn't deserve your loyalty.

GOOD SERVICE IS VALUED!

Despite the large numbers of fast-food restaurants, self-serve department stores, and pump-your-own gas stations, Americans do appreciate good service. What's more, they're willing to pay for it.

A prime example of how the American public is willing to spend extra money for better service is Federal Express, which has enjoyed immense success. For guaranteed out-of-town and/or out-of-state overnight delivery, its customers are willing to pay a premium that amounts to several thousand percent above the cost of mailing a letter. Interestingly, the majority of letters sent in the mail arrive within twenty-four hours, but there are no guarantees. I think this tells us something about Americans' appreciation for outstanding and dependable service.

I know firsthand that people are willing to pay a premium for outstanding service. Again and again, I've been told, "Joe, I shopped around before coming to see you, and I've got you beat by a hundred bucks. But I'm gonna buy from you because there's one thing nobody else can give me, and that's you, Joe." When I hear a comment of this nature, it's the most flattering compliment I could receive. Repeat sales are so easy and require little effort in comparison to the first time these customers were sold. People are truly grateful for the extra effort I put into servicing them, and they don't forget it when the time comes to buy another car. The truth is they're sold before they even walk in to see me because I've won them over by giving outstanding service the first time around.

I've read in a recent survey that in spite of some service-oriented companies' charging nearly ten percent more for their goods, their market share increased by six percentage points annually. Compare this to those companies not providing outstanding service (they lost two percentage points annually). I interpret this to mean that it *pays* to give good service, and it is certain that good service will always be appreciated by customers. Furthermore, those salespeople who give it will always outperform those who don't. Unfortunately, people don't expect it, and they're surprised when they get it. That's too bad. It should be the other way around.

THE VALUE OF A CUSTOMER

It's interesting how you come across some ideas, and how some become embedded in your mind, deeply influencing your life. Years ago I heard somebody say, "The name of the game is service. Service, service, service. Give your customers so much service they'll feel guilty even thinking about doing business with somebody else." I've never forgotten that message, and I've always lived by it. Practicing this idea has had the strongest impact on my sales career, an impact greater than any other single factor.

I've always believed that the first car I'd sell to somebody was the beginning of a long relationship. To my way of thinking, if a single car sale didn't result in future business, I considered myself a failure. To be successful in any business, it's essential to give the customer so much service that he or she will come back again and again. When you consider how many cars a satisfied customer buys during his or her lifetime, the first one is just the tip of the iceberg. I estimate that over an average car buyer's lifetime, he or she spends several hundred thousand dollars buying cars. And when I project how many friends and family members are referred by a contented customer over the years, the number runs into seven figures.

Considering the amount of money it costs a company to generate a good lead, no salesperson can afford to lose established customers because of poor servicing. One Airstream dealer, for example, calculated that his RV dealership spent an average of $85 on advertising and promotion per showroom prospect. With an average closing rate of 25 percent, the company spent $340 to obtain one customer. Add this figure to the dealership's other overhead, and it doesn't take a genius to realize the incredible waste that results from losing a customer because of poor service.

Every retail operation has an overhead that can be broken down to determine how much money is spent to get a single customer to walk through the door. Outside salespeople can also calculate what they spend to generate new business. In addition to the actual out-of-pocket costs, it is important to analyze the expense of securing new clients. In terms of the time, sweat, and blood exerted, every salesperson incurs a high intangible cost. For instance, a novice stockbroker could make as many as one hundred cold calls in a single day to generate a handful of good leads, with only one being converted into an actual order.

Real estate agents frequently canvass entire neighborhoods before a new listing is realized. And a first-year life insurance agent might make hundreds of cold calls just to obtain a single appointment. Keep in mind that's just to get to the point where he can face a warm body. If the agent's closing ratio of completed sales presentations is 20 percent, imagine how many hours of time and effort must be invested to sell just one policy.

All of this makes it clear that there's a huge expense involved in obtaining a new account, so once one is established, you can't afford to lose it. Yet, I've seen salespeople lose a customer for some of the dumbest reasons. For example, a customer brings in his new $25,000 car because his tape deck is inoperable. After it's been fixed, the dealer tells him that it's not covered under the warranty because the owner's teenagers have misused it and hands the customer a $50 repair bill. The customer begrudgingly pays, but don't count on his ever coming back. For a lousy fifty bucks, a $25,000 customer is lost! Even though the customer is wrong, you do what you have to do to please him, even if it means reaching into your own pocket. This is smart business, especially when you figure how much it costs to get a new customer. After all, it is many times more expensive to gain a brand-new customer than it is to save an old one. If you can't afford to give your customer the benefit of the doubt, I recommend cutting down on your advertising budget and putting some of the leftover money into a petty cash fund to handle minor grievances. Then you can pay for services that your customers are *not* actually entitled to receive. I assure you that by doing this, you'll be many dollars ahead.

LITTLE THINGS MAKE A BIG DIFFERENCE

Over the long run, it's the little day-to-day deeds that establish lasting salesperson-customer relationships. One of my favorite ways to build a solid rapport with my customers is by keeping in constant touch with them by mail. After a sale, I always wanted to make sure my customer would never forget me, so I developed a letter-writing program that made sure they didn't. In fact, this is what prompted somebody to say, "When you buy a car from Joe Girard, you have to leave the country to get away from the guy." Incidentally, I took that remark as a compliment.

To make sure nobody ever forgot me, every one of my customers received a letter from me every month of the year. It would arrive in a plain envelope, and I'd vary the color and size so nobody would ever know what was in it. I wanted to make sure it didn't look like that junk mail that gets thrown away before it's opened. I'd enclose a card with a message on the front saying, "I like you." Then, the inside of the card had a different message for every month of the year. January was "Happy New Year from Joe Girard"; February wished everyone "Happy Valentine's Day"; March was "Happy St. Patrick's Day"; and so on straight through to Thanksgiving and Christmas.

I never sent letters on the first or the fifteenth of the month because that's when most people receive their bills. I want to catch them in good moods. When Daddy comes home at the end of the day, the first thing he does is kiss his wife, and then he asks two questions. First, "How were the kids today?" Next he asks, "Did I get any mail today?" After the mail has been opened, the kids are shouting, "Daddy got another letter from Joe Girard!" So, as you can see, the whole family got in on the act. They love those cards, and twelve times a year my name appeared in my customers' homes in a very pleasant way. Toward the end of my career, I was sending out 14,000 cards a month. That's 168,000 a year. When you multiply that number times the cost of a first-class letter, you'll see that I was spending more on stamps than the average car salesperson makes in a year! So why was I doing it? I was doing it to tell my customers one thing: I liked them. Was it worth doing? You bet it was. Those letters were greatly responsible for the 65 percent of my sales that were repeat business each year.

When salespeople ask me how important each card was, I can't honestly answer. There's no way of knowing what effect a single letter has on anyone. How do you measure the goodwill of returning a phone call promptly, dropping off a brochure, or sending a thank-you letter to a new customer? I don't think any one of these things by itself makes a difference. After all, nobody's going to spend thousands of dollars because he or she received a Fourth of July card in the mail. But I do think the sum total of the continual performance of little thoughtful deeds makes all the difference.

I vividly recall one personal experience when I did not buy from a particular salesperson as a result of something that he undoubtedly was unaware had bothered me. I was shopping for a word processor and had telephoned to set up a one-thirty appointment with a salesman at a computer store. I arrived at one-thirty sharp, but the salesman wasn't there. It was twenty minutes later when he came prancing in.

"Sorry I'm late, Mr. Girard," he said. "What can I show you?"

"You know, if you called on me at my office and were late for an appointment, I would have enough things to keep me busy so it wouldn't upset me. But it is inexcusable for you to be late when I came to see you at *your* place of business," I said, mincing no words.

"I apologize, but you see, I was having lunch in the cafeteria in the mall across the street and the service was horrendously slow"

Your apology is not acceptable," I said. "You had an appointment with a customer, and when you sensed you were running late, you should have skipped lunch to keep your appointment. I, as a customer, not your stomach, should have been your first priority."

In spite of having a competitively priced model, there was no way he was able to close the sale because I was so aggravated about his late arrival. And the sad part about it is that I am sure he was totally oblivious as to why he didn't make the sale.

I don't think it is unusual for salespeople to lose customers because they don't follow through on what seem to be relatively unimportant matters. For this reason, if you have even the slightest hint that neglecting a minor detail might upset a customer, take care of that detail without hesitation. Roni Leeman, who sells high-priced homes in Bexley, Ohio, doesn't miss a beat when it comes to providing what appears to be a host of minor services for her clients. As you will observe from her comments, Leeman is not about to disenchant an out-of-town buyer through neglect. She says, "I'm constantly performing services for them that have nothing to do with the actual sale of real estate. For example, I serve as their information center by telling them about the educational system, schools for handicapped children, kennels for their pets, the church situation, available and reliable housekeepers, and so on. And I recommend which subcontractors to use to remodel their homes. When buyers are not in town, I'll make the arrangements with the utility companies for the turning on of their electricity, gas, water, and telephone services. Then, too, I'll meet subcontractors at the home to let them in to hang wallpaper, paint, lay carpeting, and so on I've even watered their lawns for them during a heat spell."

Leeman doesn't hesitate to spend her own money on her clients' behalf when a misunderstanding occurs. "One couple had just moved into their home and couldn't find the garage-door openers. The sellers had moved out of town, so I had to get some new ones made up for them. So what if I had to spend $150. It was a $500,000 home, and their goodwill was important to me." She explains that in the case of a large sale, buyers resent having somebody make a 6 percent commission and fail to give outstanding service. "When you pay that kind of money to a salesperson, you deserve to be treated like the queen of England," Leeman says.

CONSTANT DAY-IN-AND-DAY-OUT SERVICE

Study the truly successful American companies today and you'll discover one common theme among all of them—the great companies provide the most outstanding service in their respective industries. The IBMs, the McDonald'ses, and the American Expresses in this world always seem to end up with the lion's share of the business. Likewise, every great salesperson I've ever known has been obsessed with servicing his customers. You know the type, somewhat of a borderline fanatic who is always searching for better ways to please his or her customers. It doesn't matter what the product is, this salesperson has a constant, day-in-and-day-out desire to serve customers; the leaders in all fields are the same.

When you bombard your customers with perpetual service, you don't leave any openings for a competitor to get his or her foot in the door. Winning lifetime customers isn't based on a single mammoth act. You build ever-lasting relationships by never letting up on the servicing of your customers. By doing so, you are 'viewed as someone who is dependable because you promptly return all telephone calls, drop off brochures that were requested to be dropped off, and so on. It sounds so simple—and it is. There is nothing complicated and difficult about giving constant day-in-and-day-out service. But it does require a self-discipline that never stops.

Just the other day, while I was in the supermarket, I saw an excellent example of this kind of wonderful service. For several minutes, I watched with interest as a Frito-Lay salesman was taking what was one of his routine inventories. The salesman was painstakingly checking each shelf in the snack area to make certain there were no shortages of Frito-Lay products on the retailer's shelves. I introduced myself to him and we got into a brief conversation about servicing customers. "You wouldn't believe it, Joe," he said, "but I've driven twenty miles out of my way to restock a customer with forty-dollars' worth of potato chips."

"No kidding," I said. "How could you make money spending all that time on such a small order?"

"The company insists we give that kind of service. And your assumption is right: Driving that distance for a small order isn't worth my time. It doesn't even cover my gasoline costs. But once I get a Frito-Lay product on the shelves, I want it to stay on the shelves. In this industry, shelf space is everything. I'm not about to lose an account because it wasn't satisfied with my service."

When I got home I conducted a mini-investigation on Frito-Lay. With its 10,000+ sales force, I found out that it dominates the potato chip and pretzel industry with an estimated 70 percent market share. When you get right down to it, there is nothing much different between one manufacturer's potato chips and pretzels and its competition's. The only way a company gets that kind of market share is by having its sales reps give day-in-and-day-out service. Just like the one I saw, I'm told that all of the Frito-Lay reps are fanatics about servicing their customers. Once they get a foothold in a store, they give so much service they eventually own the account for life.

Just as a route salesman gives his best to service a grocery store account, so does International Furniture's Stan Glick, one of the nation's top furniture manufacturer's reps. Glick has built a thriving career by giving beyond-the-call-of-duty attention to detail to his retail accounts. Glick realizes the value of growing with his customers, and after the initial order he works closely with them to make sure they merchandise his line properly. Not only does he regularly take inventories, but he recommends markdowns for slow-moving goods. He routinely conducts sales meetings for his customers' sales forces, working with them on effective ways to sell his merchandise. Glick also helps create advertising by suggesting that retailers run ads that he has personally innovated and others that have been proven successful by his accounts in other cities in his territory.

And remember Larry Huttle with Airstream, whom I mentioned earlier? Huttle explains that top Airstream salespeople give a three- to five-hour demonstration *after* every sale but before the customer drives away in his newly purchased recreational vehicle. They're instructed to cover every detail of the

RV, including such minute points as how to light the hot-water heater; how to find the fuse on the microwave; how to level and set the jacks; etc. "I've seen some RV salespeople simply hand the owner's manual to a new customer and say, 'Here, read this,'" Hiittle explains. "Now there are very few people I've ever met who can figure out how to operate an RV from a manual. We want out customers to get the maximum satisfaction out of their RV because we want them to buy others from us, and we want them to refer their friends to us. A top salesman tells his customer, 'I'm on call twenty-hour hours a day. If you ever have a problem, you can call me collect at the dealership or at my home.' Our salespeople know our products well enough that when a customer has a problem, they can generally talk him through it on the phone or put him in touch with somebody in his area who can solve the problem."

It doesn't matter what you sell—potato chips, furniture, or recreational vehicles—great service is a common denominator for winning long-lasting customers. And when you give steady, reliable service and keep in constant contact with your customer, whenever a problem does occur, you can work with him to solve it. But if you only contact a customer when there is a major problem, you're in for a difficult time when you attempt to appease him. For instance, I've seen many stockbrokers call their customers only when there is something positive to report. It's easy to report good news to them, such as "XYZ is up two points today" or "It was just announced that ABC is going to make a takeover bid on XYZ." But it's equally as important for a broker to call his clients constantly to inform them of the bad news, too. "I just got a report on the wire that XYZ's earnings are off fifteen cents a share for this quarter, and I thought you should be informed." Or, "The merger with ABC fell through."

You must remember that your job isn't simply to go from sale to sale, putting all of your effort into developing new customers—you must make the time to take care of your existing customers. It's too bad, but there are many salespeople who think, "You can't make money when you service customers." At first blush, it might seem as though stopping to give service will subtract from the time you could otherwise devote to picking up new customers, but it really doesn't work that way. People do appreciate good service, and they will come back again and again to those salespeople who give it. What's more, they will send other people to you; it creates a snowball effect.

I'll repeat it once more to make sure you remember: *Service, service, service. Give your customers so much service they'll feel guilty even thinking about doing business with somebody else!* It's service like this upon which great sales careers are built, because you can go back and close sale after sale, again and again.

A FINAL MESSAGE—BE PREPARED

I have stressed the importance of being prepared before you face a customer. There are no shortcuts. It doesn't matter what you sell or where you sell it, you have to pay your dues by doing your homework. As I have printed on my business card: "The elevator to health, happiness, and success is out of order—you'll have to use the stairs—one step at a time." I hope I've emphasized this message enough times throughout this book that it is now deeply ingrained in your mind.

Knowing that it will take a lot of hard and smart work, coupled with the selling techniques and philosophies I have explained in this book, you now have the necessary tools to *close every sale—everytime!* These aren't idle words. Believe it and *you can do it*.

In my introduction, I challenged you to take my ideas and make them work even better for you than they did for me. It bears repeating—*I challenge you!*

NOTES

Chapter 2: SELLING YOURSELF

1 Robert L. Shook, *Ten Greatest Salespersons* (New York: Harper & Row, Publishers, 1978), 140.

2 Ross Perot, "How I Would Turn Around GM," *Fortune* (February 15, 1988), 49.

3 Martin Shafiroff and Robert L. Shook, *Successful Telephone Selling in the '80s* (New York: Harper & Row, Publishers, 1982), 114–15.

4 Robert L. Shook, *The Entrepreneurs* (New York: Harper & Row, Publishers, 1980), 16.

5 Ibid., 15.

6 Mary Kay Ash, *Mary Kay on People Management* (New York: Warner Books, Inc., 1984), 15.

7 Mark H. McCormack, *What They Don't Teach You at Harvard Business School* (New York: Bantam Books, 1984), 35–36.

Chapter 3: ASSUMING THE SALE

1 Robert L. Shook, *Why Didn't I Think of That!* (New York: New American Library, Inc., 1982), 127.

2 Ibid., 140.

3 Ibid., 140–41.

Chapter 8: DIFFERENT CLOSING TECHNIQUES

1 Andrew H. Thomson, *The Feldman Method* (Chicago: Farnsworth Publishing, 1969, 1980), 108.

2 Richard C. Morals, "What Is Perfume But Water and a Bit of Essence?" *Forbes* (May 2, 1988), 95.

Chapter 12: HOW TO HANDLE BUYER'S REMORSE

1 Andrew H. Thomson, *The Feldman Method* (Chicago: Farnsworth Publishing Company, 1969, 1980), 73.

2 Ibid., 73.

INDEX

About Joe Girard

Credit: bigheadstudios

JOE GIRARD is probably the most remarkable person ever to come along in the world of retail selling. Besides being the greatest retail salesperson ever, he is also one of the most gifted speakers you'll ever be in the presence of. Why? *Joe Girard has something to say.*

He always believed that working smart and being persistent could work wonders. His own life is proof positive of this. From the time he was a shoeshine boy and a newsboy growing up on Detroit's lower east side, Joe developed a keen sense of street smarts that would shock the world when he finally put them to the test on the front lines of automotive retail selling.

After numerous jobs including a dishwasher, delivery boy, stove assembler, and then a short-lived stint as a home building contractor, his fortune would change and, before long, *the whole world would know about it.*

Joe Girard joined a Chevrolet auto dealership in Eastpointe, Michigan, where he would spend the next 15 years as a new vehicle sales rep. He would go on to record an astounding and amazing career for the ages. To put it mildly, there has never been anything quite like Joe Girard before or since Joe Girard.

He has sold more retail "big ticket" items, one at a time, than any other salesperson, in any retail industry in history, including houses, boats, motor homes, insurance, automobiles, etc.

His accomplishments are simply jaw-dropping. They include no fleet, wholesale, or used car or truck sales. In addition, Joe has never held a management position! *His unbelievable sales statistics* have still not been broken!*

For the record, *this* is Joe Girard:

- Most average number of retail vehicles sold in one day—6
- Most new retail sales in one day—18
- Most new retail sales in one month—174
- Most new retail sales in one year—1,425
- Most new retail vehicles ever sold in a 15-year career—13,001
- Number one retail vehicle salesperson—12 consecutive years

Joe's awards and recognitions are as impressive as his records. He was the recipient of the coveted Golden Plate Award from the American Academy of Achievement. He was also nominated for the prestigious Horatio Alger Award by Dr. Norman Vincent Peale, author of *The Power of Positive Thinking*, and the renowned world traveler and radio broadcaster, Lowell Thomas. For his achievements, Joe Girard was inducted into the Automotive Hall of Fame in Dearborn, Michigan—the only salesperson ever to receive this honor. He is listed in the *Guinness Book of World Records* as the "World's Greatest Salesman".

He remains one of the world's most electrifying motivational speakers and has an enviable portfolio of important clients including Harvard Business School, 3M, Brunswick Corporation, CBS Records, Allstate Insurance, Ford Motor Company, General Electric, General Motors, Hewlett-Packard, IBM, John Deere, Mary Kay Cosmetics, and Bell Canada, just to name a few.

Joe has authored 5 multimillion selling books on sales leadership and self improvement:

How To Sell Anything To Anybody
How To Sell Yourself
How To Close Every Sale
Mastering Your Way To The Top
Life's 13 Rules
www.joegirard.com

* All statistics audited and confirmed by the accounting firm, Deloitte & Touche. Audit available upon request.